OCR SHP GCSE

LIVING UNDER NAZI RULE

1933–1945

RICHARD KENNETT

SERIES EDITORS:
Jamie Byrom and Michael Riley

The Schools History Project

Set up in 1972 to bring new life to history for school students, the Schools History Project has been based at Leeds Trinity University since 1978. SHP continues to play an innovatory role in history education based on its six principles:

- Making history meaningful for young people
- Engaging in historical enquiry
- Developing broad and deep knowledge
- Studying the historic environment
- Promoting diversity and inclusion
- Supporting rigorous and enjoyable learning

These principles are embedded in the resources which SHP produces in partnership with Hodder Education to support history at Key Stage 3, GCSE (SHP OCR B) and A level. The Schools History Project contributes to national debate about school history. It strives to challenge, support and inspire teachers through its published resources, conferences and website: **http://www.schoolshistoryproject.org.uk**

This resource is endorsed by OCR for use with specification OCR Level 1/2 GCSE (9–1) in History B (Schools History Project) (J411). In order to gain OCR endorsement, this resource has undergone an independent quality check. Any references to assessment and/or assessment preparation are the publisher's interpretation of the specification requirements and are not endorsed by OCR. OCR recommends that a range of teaching and learning resources are used in preparing learners for assessment. OCR has not paid for the production of this resource, nor does OCR receive any royalties from its sale. For more information about the endorsement process, please visit the OCR website, www.ocr.co.uk.

The publishers thank OCR for permission to use specimen exam questions on pages 101–104 from OCR's GCSE (9–1) History B (Schools History Project) © OCR 2016. OCR has neither seen nor commented upon any model answers or exam guidance related to these questions.

Note: The wording and sentence structure of some written sources have been adapted and simplified to make them accessible to all pupils while faithfully preserving the sense of the original.

Every effort has been made to trace all copyright holders, but if any have been inadvertently overlooked, the Publishers will be pleased to make the necessary arrangements at the first opportunity.

Although every effort has been made to ensure that website addresses are correct at time of going to press, Hodder Education cannot be held responsible for the content of any website mentioned in this book. It is sometimes possible to find a relocated web page by typing in the address of the home page for a website in the URL window of your browser.

Hachette UK's policy is to use papers that are natural, renewable and recyclable products and made from wood grown in sustainable forests. The logging and manufacturing processes are expected to conform to the environmental regulations of the country of origin.

Orders: please contact Bookpoint Ltd, 130 Park Drive, Milton Park, Abingdon, Oxon OX14 4SE. Telephone: (44) 01235 827720. Fax: (44) 01235 400454. Email: education@bookpoint.co.uk Lines are open from 9 a.m. to 5 p.m., Monday to Saturday, with a 24-hour message answering service. You can also order through our website: www.hoddereducation.co.uk

ISBN: 978 1 4718 6092 8

© Richard Kennett 2017

First published in 2017 by
Hodder Education
An Hachette UK Company
Carmelite House
50 Victoria Embankment
London EC4Y 0DZ

www.hoddereducation.co.uk

Impression number   10 9 8 7 6 5 4 3 2

Year   2021 2020 2019 2018 2017

Cover photo © Glasshouse Images/Alamy Stock Photo

Typeset by White-Thomson Publishing LTD

Printed in Dubai

A catalogue record for this title is available from the British Library.

CONTENTS

INTRODUCTION

Making the most of this book

 Where this book fits into your GCSE history course

The course

The GCSE history course you are following is made up of five different studies. These are shown in the table below. For each type of study you will follow one option. We have highlighted the option that this particular book helps you with.

OCR SHP GCSE B
(Choose one option from each section)

Paper 1 1 ¾ hours	**British thematic study** ● The People's Health ● Crime and Punishment ● Migrants to Britain	**20%**
	British depth study ● The Norman Conquest ● Elizabethan England ● Britain in Peace and War	**20%**
Paper 2 1 hour	**History around us** ● Any site that meets the given criteria.	**20%**
Paper 3 1 ¾ hours	**World period study** ● Viking Expansion ● The Mughal Empire ● The Making of America	**20%**
	World depth study ● The First Crusade ● The Aztecs and the Spanish Conquest ● Living under Nazi Rule	**20%**

The world depth study

The world depth study focuses on a traumatic short period in world history when different cultures or ideologies were in conflict. It encourages you to engage with many rich, contemporary sources and the different interpretations of historians. As you do this you will learn about the nature of historical evidence and how history is constructed.

As the table shows, you will be examined on your knowledge and understanding of the world depth study as part of Paper 3. You can find out more about that on pages 98–105 at the back of the book.

Here is exactly what the specification shows for this depth study.

Living under Nazi Rule, 1933–45

The specification divides this period into five sections:

Sections	Learners should study the following content:
Dictatorship	• Hitler and the Nazi Party in January 1933 • Establishing the dictatorship, January 1933 to July 1933 • Achieving total power, July 1933 to August 1934
Control and opposition, 1933–39	• The machinery of terror including the SS, the law courts, concentration camps and the Gestapo • The range and effectiveness of Nazi propaganda • Opposition to Nazi rule including the Left, Church leaders and youth groups
Changing lives, 1933–39	• Work and home: the impact of Nazi policies on men and women • The lives of young people in Nazi Germany including education and youth movements • Nazi racial policy: the growing persecution of Jews
Germany in war	• The move to a war economy and its impact on the German people, 1939–42 • Growing opposition from the German people including from elements within the army • The impact of total war on the German people, 1943–45
Occupation	• The contrasting nature of Nazi rule in eastern and western Europe • The Holocaust, including the *Einsatzgruppen*, ghettos and the death camps • Responses to Nazi rule: collaboration, accommodation and resistance

You need to understand the interplay between these forces in society:

● Political
● Economic
● Social
● Racial
● Cultural

You also need to understand:

● the impact of the Nazi dictatorship on people's lives within Germany and across occupied Europe
● the diverse lives and experiences of people during this traumatic time.

In addition, you should be able to:

● engage with a range of historical sources
● understand different interpretations of aspects of life under Nazi rule.

The next two pages show how this book works.

How this book works

The rest of this book (from pages 8 to 97) is carefully arranged to match what the specification requires. It does this through the following features:

Enquiries

The book is largely taken up with five 'enquiries'. Each enquiry sets you a challenge in the form of an overarching question.

The first two pages of the enquiry set up the challenge and give you a clear sense of what you will need to do to work out your answer to the main question. You will find the instructions set out in 'The Enquiry' box, on a blue background, as in this example.

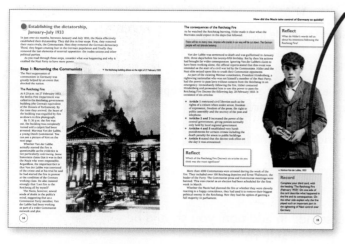

Record tasks

From that point, the enquiry is divided into three sections. These match the bullet points shown in the specification on page 3. You can tell when you are starting a new section as it will start with a large coloured heading like the one shown here. Throughout each section there are 'Record' tasks, where you will be asked to record ideas and information that will help you make up your mind about the overarching enquiry question later on. You can see an example of these 'Record' instructions here. They will always be in blue text with blue lines above and below them.

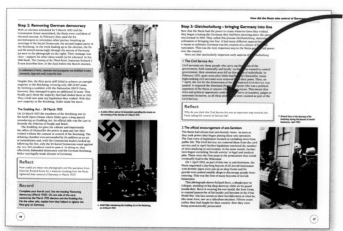

Reflect tasks

At regular intervals we will set a 'Reflect' task to prompt you to think carefully about what you are reading. They will look like the examples shown here. These Reflect tasks help you to check that what you are reading is making sense and to see how it connects with what you have already learned. You do not need to write down the ideas that you think of when you 'reflect', but the ideas you get may help you when you reach the next Record instruction.

Review tasks

Each enquiry ends by asking you to review what
you have been learning and use it to answer the
overarching question in some way. Sometimes you
simply answer that one question. Sometimes you will
need to do two or three tasks that each tackle some
aspect of the main question. The important point is
that you should be able to use the ideas and evidence
you have been building up through the enquiry to
support your answer.

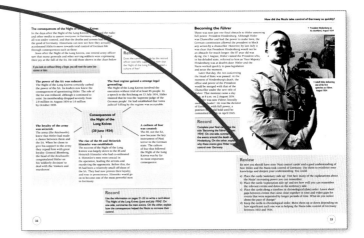

Closer looks

Between the enquiries you will find pages that provide
a 'closer look' at some aspect of the theme or period
you are studying. These will often give you a chance
to find out more about the issue you have just been
studying in the previous enquiry, although they may
sometimes look ahead to the next enquiry.

We may not include any tasks within these 'closer
looks' but, as you read them, keep thinking of what
they add to your knowledge and understanding. We
think they add some intriguing insights.

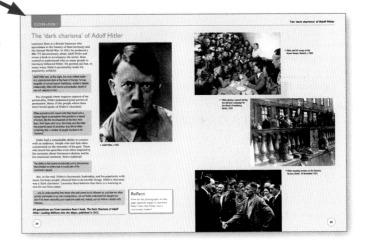

One very important final point

We have chosen enquiry questions that should help you get to the really
important issues at the heart of each period you study, but you need to
remember that the examiners will almost certainly ask you different
questions when you take your GCSE. Don't simply rely on the notes you
made to answer the enquiry questions we gave you. We give you advice on
how to tackle the examination and the different sorts of question you will
face on pages 98 to 105.

● Hitler's 'struggle' before 1933

Mein Kampf, meaning 'my struggle', was first published in two volumes in 1925 and 1926. It was largely written from a prison cell, by Adolf Hitler, an ex-corporal in the German army that had lost the First World War in 1918.

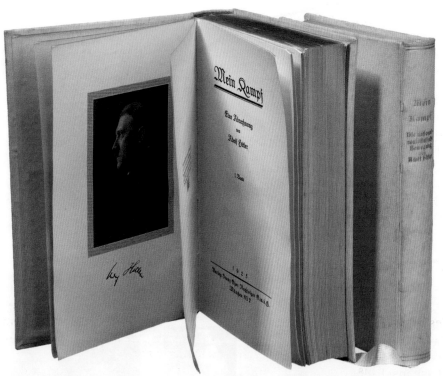

▲ A first edition of Adolf Hitler's two-volume book, *Mein Kampf*, 1926

Early years, 1889–1923

Hitler was born into a poor Austrian family in 1889. As a child he became fascinated with the idea that all German-speaking people, such as the Austrians, should really belong to a single great German nation. By 1913, he had moved to the capital of southern Germany, Munich. It was there that he joined the German army to fight in the First World War from 1914 to 1918.

When Germany lost the war Hitler felt very bitter in defeat. Like many other Germans, he believed that the politicians who had taken over the country at the very end of the war had given in too easily. In particular, Hitler believed that powerful and cowardly Jews, many of whom were also communists, had swayed the government's decision. There is no historical evidence to support this explanation but in the post-war years in Germany it became a popular way of accounting for the army's sudden defeat in 1918. In a similar way, Hitler and many other Germans blamed the politicians for accepting too readily the severe peace settlement that was part of the 1919 Treaty of Versailles.

Hitler drifted around Munich after the war, seeking friends who, like him, took a very right-wing view of politics. In 1920, he became the leader of a tiny, extreme right-wing party that had just decided to call itself the National Socialist German Workers Party. It stood for nationalism (the greatness of a single nation for all German-speaking people) and for the social needs of the workers in their daily lives. Its German name was the *Nationalsozialistische Deutsche Arbeiterpartei* but its members called themselves the shortened name: the Nazis.

Early failure

In November 1923, Hitler led his Nazi Party in an attempt to seize power over southern Germany by launching an armed attack on the government. This *Munich Putsch* failed completely. Hitler was captured and given a fairly light prison sentence that he served in a large, comfortable room in a German castle. In his captivity, Hitler decided that he would no longer try to gain power by force. Instead he would exploit German democratic processes to win elections. Once he was in charge of an elected Nazi government, he would use the full power of the state to shape the country as he wished.

While he was in the castle, Hitler started to write about his 'struggle' in life so far ... and where he wanted it to lead in the years ahead. These were the ideas that he set out in the long-winded, rambling and extremist text of *Mein Kampf*.

Eventual success

In *Mein Kampf* and in his speeches throughout the 1920s, Hitler made his intentions clear:

- The Nazis must **get into power legally**, not by a violent takeover. In order to do this, they would build mass support by making generous promises.
- Once elected to power, the Nazis would **end all opposition**, as Germany needed the strength of a single-party government.
- **Purify Germany** by removing any Jewish influence. If necessary, the Jews must be deported ... or removed by other means.
- **Strengthen Germany's economy and armed forces** so that the nation could once again dominate Europe, even if this meant breaking the terms set out in the Treaty of Versailles.
- **Germany must gain land** by fighting and winning another war to recapture areas lost through the Treaty of Versailles (for example, to Poland) and to gain whole regions of eastern Europe that would give the German people the living space (*Lebensraum*) that they needed to thrive.
- The Nazis must, by these policies, set up and pass on to later generations of Germans **a great empire (Reich)**. There had been two such great German empires before 1918, so this one would be called the 'Third Reich' and it would last for a thousand years.

Between 1924 and 1933, Hitler and his Nazis campaigned in elections, promising to do exactly what had been outlined in *Mein Kampf*. Through a mix of political cunning, weak opposition, lies and brute force, the Nazis had achieved their first aim by 30 January 1933: that was when Adolf Hitler became the new Chancellor (Prime Minister) of Germany. This photograph shows the Nazi Party celebrations that filled the capital city of Berlin that night. In the days, months and years that followed, Hitler and the Nazis set about implementing their other plans for Germany – no matter what the cost in human life and suffering. The rest of this book tells that story.

◄ Crowds of Nazi supporters celebrate in Berlin on 30 January 1933. The Nazis' private army, known as the SA, is leading a torchlight march through the streets as spotlights shine on the masses.

Democracy to dictatorship

How were the Nazis able to take control of Germany so quickly?

This photograph shows Adolf Hitler walking up the stairs at the Nazi Party rally in Nuremberg in September 1934. He is receiving rapturous applause and adulation from the 700,000 supporters.

By this time Hitler was *der Führer*, the dictator who ruled all aspects of German life. His Nazi dictatorship could make whatever laws it wished as it had completely removed all democracy and any other threat to its power. This brutal and total control lasted until 1945.

Yet if we rewind to January 1933 things looked very different, and total power was far from inevitable. Hitler had just been made Chancellor (similar to Prime Minister) but he still had many obstacles to overcome before he could establish the Nazi dictatorship he dreamed of:

- As Chancellor, Hitler was not the most powerful man in Germany. That was the President, Paul von Hindenburg.
- Germany in 1933 was a democracy. Although the Nazi Party was the largest party in the Reichstag (the German Parliament) it did not have a majority of seats so it needed the consent of others to pass any laws.
- Although the Nazis were the largest party in the Reichstag, they only had 37 per cent of the votes, meaning over 60 per cent of the population did not fully agree with their ideas.
- There were many individuals and groups in German society who detested the Nazis and their ideas.
- There was a real danger of a power struggle within the Nazi Party that could endanger Hitler's position as leader.

The Enquiry

Your challenge in this enquiry is to work out how Hitler and the Nazis overcame these obstacles to take total control of Germany within 18 months. The enquiry examines the process in three phases:

1. Hitler and the Nazi Party in January 1933
2. Establishing the dictatorship between January 1933 and July 1933
3. Achieving total power between July 1933 and August 1934

As you move through the enquiry you will be making nine 'Nazi control cards'.

On one side of each card you will describe an event that helped Hitler and the Nazis take control. On the other side you will explain *how* the event helped them to tighten their grip on Germany.

At the end of the enquiry you will use your pack of cards to develop and organise your knowledge and understanding of this crucial phase in the history of Germany.

◀ Adolf Hitler at the Nuremberg Nazi Party rally, 1934

Hitler and the Nazi Party in January 1933

The Nazi Party in January 1933 was an effective political force. This had not always been the case. As you learned on pages 6 and 7, throughout the 1920s the Nazis had struggled to win any significant support from voters. In the late 1920s, however, the party reorganised itself to great effect. In 1932 they had won the largest percentage of seats in the Reichstag and had a membership of over 850,000 people.

Nazi leaders in 1933

Although Hitler was undoubtedly the dominant figure in the Nazi Party, he was well-supported by a group of intense and committed leaders.

At the head of the party was **Adolf Hitler**. Hitler had been the party leader since 1921 and was instrumental in its success. A very charismatic speaker who could captivate a large crowd, he was a nationally known figure. Jailed for attempting to take power by force in 1923, Hitler was hailed at his trial by the press for his strong opinions. While in prison he wrote *Mein Kampf* (*My Struggle*), which clearly set out his racist and nationalistic views. It went on to be a national bestseller. In 1932 during the election he used an aeroplane to fly around Germany delivering speeches. He was the central figure in the Nazi Party structure.

Nazi ideas were spread far and wide by the party's propaganda team, co-ordinated by **Joseph Goebbels**. As a highly educated man from the middle classes, he realised the power of modern media and utilised posters, newspapers and new technology in the forms of radio and film. Goebbels used simple, bold messages to make a point. During the Great Depression, for example, the Nazis had fought the election on the campaign motto 'bread and work', appealing to the two basic demands of the needy population. He had deeply anti-Semitic ideas. His propaganda also emphasised the strength of Hitler who was portrayed as a god-like supreme being.

Wilhelm Frick was a long-standing member of the party. In 1933, when Hitler was made Chancellor, only two other Nazis were given roles in the Cabinet: Göring was one and Frick was the other. He was made Minister of the Interior, with overall responsibility for most aspects of life in German society. From 1930 to 1931, he had experience of high office in one of Germany's state parliaments where he used his powers to promote Nazis into important positions and to spread Nazi ideas in schools. Frick helped to shape the party's racial policy.

Nazi leaders in 1933

Ernst Röhm was the leader of the SA (short for *Sturmabteilung* or Storm Department, but more commonly known as 'brownshirts'). Originally set up as bodyguards for Hitler, the SA had turned into the Nazi's private army. Röhm took charge of the SA in 1930 and greatly increased its strength so that it had 400,000 'stormtroopers' by 1933. These were used to intimidate voters and other political parties. During the election they stood outside polling booths and intimidating voters into voting for the Nazis. They also physically attacked Communists.

Hermann Göring, an ex-First World War fighter pilot, was second in power to Hitler. He joined the German Cabinet along with Frick and Hitler in 1933. He had no clear role at first but he helped the party to run smoothly. Before long, his government responsibilities included controlling the police in Prussia, the largest German region. In 1933, Göring formed the Gestapo, the Nazi secret police that would spy on the German people to stop opposition to the party.

Rudolph Hess, another ex-First World War hero, was third in power to Hitler. He was Deputy Leader of the party and it was his job to sign off all new legislation to ensure that it closely followed the Nazi ideology. He worked in Munich at the headquarters of the party and made certain everyone was following the same goals.

Heinrich Himmler led the SS (*Schutzstaffel* or Protection Squadron, more commonly known as 'blackshirts'). This, like the SA, had started as a group of Nazi volunteers who provided security for party leaders. By the end of 1933, the SS had about 200,000 members. Its 'elite guard' was a paramilitary force with strict entrance requirements whose members were fanatical about Nazi ideology. They numbered over 50,000 and, under Himmler, were developing the methods of surveillance and terror that would later gain them notoriety. The SS would go on to be one of the defining features of Nazi Germany, running the concentration camps, spying on its people and striking fear into the hearts of anyone living under a Nazi-led regime.

Record

At the top of your first card write 'Leadership of the Nazi Party (January 1933)'. On the front of the card list the names of each of these seven leaders and very briefly summarise the role of each one. On the back explain why the skills and personalities of these people helped the Nazis to increase their control.

Nazi ideology in 1933

◀ A German
schoolroom
in 1933

This photograph was taken in a German school in 1933. It shows an event especially arranged by the Nazi Party. A group of schoolgirls is being taught what happened to Germany after its defeat in the 1914–18 war. They are learning how Great Britain, France and the USA imposed harsh terms on Germany in the Treaty of Versailles in 1919. This treaty:

- severely restricted German armed forces (for example, they were only allowed an army of 100,000 soldiers)
- reduced German territories
- imposed a crippling bill of £6.6 billion that the Germans owed to repair the damage they had caused throughout Europe.

Students were also taught how the Treaty of Versailles cast a dark shadow over Germany from 1918 until Hitler took power in January 1933. In those years, Germany was ruled by what became known as the 'Weimar Government'. Despite some real signs of hope and recovery in the mid 1920s, these were grim years for most German people.

Many Germans blamed the Weimar politicians for failing to end their problems. Extreme left- and right-wing political parties put forward wildly different solutions and clashed in outbursts of street violence. The economy suffered terribly as German industry and farming struggled to overcome problems caused by the Treaty of Versailles and then by the worldwide Great Depression that ruined trade in the early 1930s. Unemployment was high and wages were low.

It was during these years that the Nazis first spread their own ideology (ideas and beliefs). You can get a sense of these from the list of Nazi demands on page 13.

Reflect

What does the photograph tell us about education in Germany after the Nazis gained power in 1933?

Record

Use pages 12 and 13 to make a 'control card' about 'Nazi ideology (January 1933)'. On one side describe the key Nazi ideas in 1933. You can't write about them all, so choose three or four that you think were most important, considering the context of the time. On the back of the card explain why these ideas would have helped the Nazi Party build its support so easily in the following year.

The main Nazi demands

- **Scrap the Treaty of Versailles**: the Nazis believed that Germany should ignore the harsh restrictions placed on it by the Allies, especially those that restricted the armed forces. They also wanted to take back former German lands that had been given to nations such as Poland.
- *Brot und Arbeit* ('Bread and Work' for all): these bare necessities were promised to all unemployed Germans so that their needs would be met and the German people would be more united and contented.
- **Destroy Marxism**: Marxism is a type of communism. The Bolsheviks (a Marxist party) had led the communist revolution in Russia in 1917. According to the Nazis, the Bolsheviks were led by Jews. They needed to be stopped so that they could not stir up a similar communist revolution in Germany.
- **Subdue the Jews**: Nazi ideas were fuelled by anti-Semitism. This means that they saw Jews as *Untermenschen* (sub-humans). Jews were blamed as the cowards who had made Germany surrender in 1918, as the communists who had plotted revolution and as the money-grabbers who had benefitted at the expense of the poor.
- **Ensure Aryan supremacy**: the Nazis believed that northern Europeans were *Übermenschen* (super humans); they called the Slavs of eastern Europe *Düngervolk* (dung-people). The ideal Aryan had blond hair and blue eyes but northern Europeans without these features could still be considered Aryan.
- **Fight for *Lebensraum*** (living space): *Lebensraum* was needed to grow the food that the German people needed. The Nazis wanted to take large parts of eastern Europe by force, believing that it was wasted on the Slavs who lived there.
- **Build Nationalism**: the Nazi extreme form of patriotism included the belief that Germany should be run by Germans for Germans. The Nazis believed that foreign influence, or the involvement of non-Aryans, especially Jews, should be removed from society.
- **Strengthen central government**: in Germany there was a tradition of local government having lots of power to make decisions. The Nazis believed that this should be removed and the power of the central national government should be increased.
- **Nationalise important industries**: the Nazis believed that services, such as the supply of electricity, water and railway transport, should be provided by the government for the good of the nation rather than by independent companies for private profit.
- **Improve education**: education was seen by the Nazis as crucial to improving the economy. They believed that Germans needed an improved education system so that the German people could work more efficiently, make Germany strong again and learn to accept Nazi ideology.

These ideas and beliefs made a powerful blend. Relatively few Germans accepted all of them but there was something in Nazi ideology that appealed to many members of the population. Here is how one farmer described his own response to the Nazis in 1934:

From *Why I Became a Nazi*, written in 1934. The author was a farmer who had fought in the First World War.

[After November 1918] ... the consequences of the betrayal of the nation became more and more evident. ... The Jew was at fault for all our misery. [In the 1920s] ... we all shared the same desire to wipe out the existing system which had come to power by betrayal of the people and country. We wanted ... no social groups and classes but only the German people.

The Leader spoke of the threatened ruin of our nation and of the resurrection under the Third Reich. How insignificant had all parties become to my eyes. How despicable was communism. [Hitler] gave us faith in the German people. If we won, Germany was saved; if we were defeated, a gate would open up and Moscow's Red (communist) hordes would swarm in and plunge Europe into a night of misery.

Reflect

1. Which aspects of Nazi ideology have obviously appealed to this German farmer?
2. There are other aspects of the list above that the German farmer did not refer to. Does this mean that he was not a true Nazi?

Establishing the dictatorship, January–July 1933

In just over six months, between January and July 1933, the Nazis effectively established their dictatorship. They did this in four steps. First, they removed their main rivals, the Communists. Next they removed the German democracy. Third, they began creating fear in the German population and finally they removed the last elements of external opposition: the trades unions and other political parties.

As you read through these steps, consider what was happening and why it enabled the Nazi Party to have more power.

Step 1: Removing the Communists

▼ The Reichstag building ablaze on the night of 27 February 1933

The Nazi suppression of communism in Germany was greatly helped by an event that shocked the nation.

The Reichstag Fire

At 9.25 p.m. on 27 February 1933, the Berlin Fire Department was called to the Reichstag government building (the German equivalent of the Houses of Parliament). By the time they arrived, the heart of the building was engulfed by fire as shown in this photograph.

By 11.30 p.m. the fire was out, the building was completely ruined and a culprit had been arrested: Marinus Van der Lubbe, a young Dutch Communist. You can see a picture of him on the next page.

Whether Van der Lubbe actually started the fire is questionable as the evidence is not particularly convincing. Some historians claim that it was in fact the Nazis who were responsible. Regardless, the important fact is that Van der Lubbe was convicted of the crime and at his trial he said he had started the fire in protest at the condition of the German working class. He also insisted strongly that 'I set fire to the Reichstag all by myself'.

The Nazis, however, sowed seeds of doubt in the public's mind, suggesting that as a Communist Party member, Van der Lubbe had been working as part of a wider Communist network and plot.

The consequences of the Reichstag Fire

As he watched the Reichstag burning, Hitler made it clear what the Marxists could expect in the days that followed:

> There will be no mercy now. Anyone who stands in our way will be cut down. The German people will not tolerate leniency.

Van der Lubbe was sentenced to death and was guillotined in January 1934, three days before his twenty-fifth birthday. But by then his actions had brought far wider consequences. Ignoring Van der Lubbe's claim to have been working alone, the official reports stated that this event was intended as the start of a civil war led by the Communists. Hitler and the Nazi elite seized upon this to crush their Communist opponents.

As part of the existing Weimar constitution, President Hindenburg, a right-wing nationalist who was not himself a member of the Nazi Party, had the power to pass laws without consent from the Reichstag in an emergency. Immediately following the fire, Hitler contacted Hindenburg and persuaded him to use this power to pass the Reichstag Fire Decree the following day, 28 February 1933. It consisted of six articles:

- **Article 1** restricted civil liberties such as the rights of a citizen when under arrest, freedom of expression, freedom of the press, the right to public assembly and the secrecy of the post and telephone.
- **Articles 2 and 3** increased the power of the central government, giving powers normally only held by local regional government.
- **Articles 4 and 5** established very harsh punishments for certain crimes including the death penalty for arson to public buildings.
- **Article 6** stated that the decree took effect on the day it was announced.

Reflect

Which of the Reichstag Fire Decree's six articles do you think was the most significant?

More than 4000 Communists were arrested during the week of the fire. They included over 100 Reichstag deputies and Ernst Thälmann, the leader of the Party. The Communist press and Communist meetings were banned. This was crucial as an election had been scheduled for the first week in March.

Whether the Nazis had planned the fire or whether they were cleverly reacting to a coincidence, they had used it to remove their biggest political enemy in the Reichstag. Now they had the option of gaining a full majority in parliament.

Reflect

What do Hitler's words tell us about his intentions following the Reichstag Fire?

▲ Marinus Van der Lubbe, 1933

Record

Complete your third card, with the heading 'The Reichstag Fire (February 1933)'. On one side of the card describe what happened in the fire and its consequences. On the other side explain why the fire played such an important part in the tightening of Nazi control over Germany.

Step 2: Removing German democracy

With an election scheduled for 5 March 1933 and the Communist threat neutralised, the Nazis were confident of electoral success. In February they used the SA stormtroopers to intimidate other parties, breaking up meetings of the Social Democrats, the second largest party in the Reichstag. In the week leading up to the election, the SA and SS moved menacingly through the streets of Germany (as seen in the photograph on the right). Their message was clear – support for other ideas would not be tolerated. In his 2004 book, *The Coming of the Third Reich*, historian Richard J. Evans describes how, in the days before the March election,

> A combination of terror, repression and propaganda was mobilized in every community, large and small, across the land.

Despite this, the Nazi party still failed to achieve an outright majority in the Reichstag, winning only 288 of 647 seats. By forming a coalition with the Nationalist DNVP Party, however, they managed to gain an additional 52 seats. This finally gave them the majority that had eluded them in 1932. They could now pass any legislation they wished. With this new majority in the Reichstag, Hitler made his move.

The Enabling Act – 24 March 1933

On 24 March 1933 the members of the Reichstag met in the Kroll Opera House where Hitler gave a long speech introducing an Enabling Act. Its official title was the Law to Remedy the Distress of People and Reich.

The Enabling Act gave the cabinet and importantly the office of Chancellor the power to pass any law they wished without the consent or control of the Reichstag. The debating chamber was surrounded by SA soldiers as an act of intimidation and, with the Communist leaders locked up following the fire, only the 94 Social Democrats voted against the Act; 444 members voted to pass it. In doing so, they effectively disbanded democracy and the German Reichstag. Hitler was legally made dictator of Germany.

▲ A police officer and an SA brownshirt patrolling the streets on the morning of the election of 5 March 1933

▲ Adolf Hitler introducing the Enabling Act in the Reichstag, 24 March 1933

Reflect

How useful are these two photographs and the quotation from historian Richard J. Evans for a historian studying how the Nazis tightened their control of Germany in March 1933?

Record

Complete your fourth card. Use the heading 'Removing democracy (March 1933)'. On one side of the card, summarise the March 1933 election and the Enabling Act. On the other side, explain how they helped to tighten the Nazi grip on Germany.

Step 3: *Gleichschaltung* – bringing Germany into line

Now that the Nazis had the power to create whatever laws they wished, they began creating the Germany they had been planning since the party was formed in 1919. They called this process *Gleichschaltung*, meaning co-ordination or bringing into line. It had many different aspects but what it meant to ordinary Germans was the creation of a culture of fear and repression. This was the next important step in the Nazis gaining full power over the country.

Here are four particularly important early aspects of *Gleichschaltung*:

1 The Civil Service Act

Civil servants are those people who carry out the duties of the government, both nationally and locally. As the Nazis wanted to control government, their attention soon fell on this group of individuals. In February 1933, quite soon after Hitler had become Chancellor, many high-ranking civil servants were removed from their posts. Then, on 7 April, the Act for the Restoration of the Professional Civil Service was passed. It required the dismissal (firing) of anyone who was a political opponent of the Nazis or anyone who was non-Aryan. This meant that Jews and political opponents could no longer serve as teachers, judges or university lecturers, as all these professions were counted as part of the Civil Service.

Reflect

Why do you think this Civil Service Act was an important step towards the Nazis taking full control of German life?

▼ Richard Stern in the doorway of his bookshop during the boycott of Jewish businesses, April 1933

2 The official encouragement of anti-Semitism

The Nazis had always had anti-Semitic views. As soon as they took power they began putting these into operation. The first wave of legislation focused on excluding Jews from public life. The Civil Service Act removed them from the civil service and in April further legislation restricted the number of Jews studying in universities. In the same month, further laws began curtailing 'Jewish activity' in legal and medical jobs. These were the first steps in the persecution that would eventually lead to the Holocaust.

On 1 April 1933, as part of this rise in anti-Semitism, the Nazis organised a day-long boycott of all Jewish businesses. Anti-Semitic signs were put up on shop fronts and SA guards were posted outside shops to discourage people from entering. This was the first of many boycotts of Jewish businesses.

This photograph shows Richard Stern, a shopkeeper in Cologne, standing in his shop doorway while an SA guard stands duty. Stern is wearing his war medal, the Iron Cross, to remind passers-by of his loyalty and heroism in the First World War. His face seems to show bewilderment at what he, like most Jews, saw as a ridiculous situation. Fifteen years earlier they had fought for their country. Now they were being systematically persecuted.

3 Book burning

The Nazis did not want to just bring people into line according to party or race: they also wanted to control ideas. Encouraged by Goebbels' Propaganda Ministry, Nazi student groups were urged to take part in action against what was called 'Un-German Spirit'. On 10 May 1933 in university cities across Germany, Nazi students burnt 25,000 volumes of 'un-German' books. These included works by Jewish and Communist authors or anyone else whom the Nazis deemed to be un-German.

> **Speaking at the book burning in Berlin on 10 May 1933, Joseph Goebbels, Reich Minister for Public Enlightenment and Propaganda, declared:**
>
> German men and women! The age of arrogant Jewish intellectualism is now at an end! … You are doing the right thing at this midnight hour – to consign to the flames the unclean spirit of the past. This is a great, powerful, and symbolic act. … Out of these ashes the phoenix of a new age will arise. … Oh Century! Oh Science! It is a joy to be alive!

▲ Members of the SA and students burning books, 1933

4 The use of terror

In 1933, the Nazis turned their full force against their opponents. Jews, Communists, Social Democrats and trades unions all faced the wrath of the SA and the SS. It is difficult to know exact numbers but most historians believe that up to 600 were murdered in 1933 and, by October of that year, over 100,000 had been arrested. Many of these people were imprisoned in concentration camps, which were set up all over Germany, the first being at Dachau in March 1933.

The SA became increasingly violent. In June 1933, in what has become known as the Köpenick Week of Blood, a Social Democrat shot three SA stormtroopers. In retaliation, the SA arrested 500 men and tortured them so severely that 91 died.

▲ Nazi opponents being arrested, 1933

Reflect

1. What do you notice about the pace of change in the first six months of 1933?
2. What does this suggest about the Nazis?

Record

Use pages 17 and 18 to complete your fifth card using the heading '*Gleichschaltung* (February to July 1933)'. On one side, summarise, with specific evidence, the most important changes imposed by the Nazis in these months. On the reverse, explain why this enabled the Nazis to gain tighter control.

Step 4: Removing opposition

By late spring in 1933, the power of the Nazi Party and the government had increased considerably but there were still two non-Nazi groups of potential opponents – other political parties and the trades unions. In the four months leading up to July 1933, both these threats were systematically removed.

Trades unions

Trades unions are set up to protect the rights of workers, fighting for better pay and conditions. They are traditionally very left wing and, as a result, the majority of the unionists in 1933 were against the Nazi Party and their ideology.

In February 1933, fearing that trades unions would organise a strike to demonstrate their opposition, the Nazis arrested the main union leaders. The remaining leaders felt that the only workable option was to co-operate with the Nazis rather than work against them. They met Goebbels to see if a compromise could be agreed between the two groups. Goebbels promised all workers an annual holiday in honour of German labour, which pleased the union leaders.

The Day of National Labour on 1 May was a great success with over a million crowding on to Tempelhof airfield in Berlin to hear leading Nazis speak. However, the trades union leaders had been duped. On 2 May, the offices of every left-wing trades union were raided, the leaders arrested and their newspapers shut down. Assets and membership were put under the control of the Nazi-led German Labour Front (DAF). (For more details about the DAF see page 47.)

Other political parties

Although the Enabling Act made the Reichstag redundant, as the Nazis could make laws without it, other political parties still existed and began complaining about the Nazi changes.

The Social Democrats (SD) had been the largest party before 1932 and once the trades unions were removed they became the next Nazi target. On 10 May, the Nazis claimed that there had been corrupt use of SD funds and so seized all SD offices and wealth, with many leaders fleeing as a result. On 21 June, Frick used an emergency decree to ban the Social Democrats as a 'dangerous enemy'. In total, 3000 party workers were arrested, imprisoned and tortured.

Once other parties saw this, they knew a similar fate awaited them. Rather than be arrested, one by one the remaining parties dissolved themselves (shut themselves down) in late June and early July.

On 14 July 1933, the Act to Ban New Parties was passed. The Nazis were now running a one-party state with no official opposition. You might imagine that Hitler would have been satisfied but, as you will see, he soon turned his attention to crushing disloyalty and any hint of opposition inside his own Nazi ranks.

◀ Mass support for Hitler and the Nazi Party at a Labour Day event in the Lustgarten, Berlin, May 1933

Record

Complete your sixth card. Use the title 'Removing external opposition (May to July 1933)'. On one side, summarise how the Nazis removed the threat from trades unions and other political parties. On the other, explain why this increased the Nazis' hold on Germany.

Achieving total power, July 1933 to August 1934

In July 1933, Hitler gathered the leading Nazis together and told them that:

> The stream of revolution has been undammed, but it must be channelled into the secure bed of evolution.

He was saying that steps taken in his first six months as Chancellor had released a flood of changes but that the time had come to consolidate Nazi power. This was done throughout the following year, from July 1933 to August 1934.

Further legislation

Two of the most significant new acts passed in this time gave the Nazis effective control of local government and of Germany's justice system.

Controlling local government

Local government in Germany was organised into regions, or *Länder*. Each region could elect its own assembly to manage local affairs. The Nazis could not tolerate this, as it was a part of the government system outside their control. During 1933, power had slowly been removed from the regions but in January 1934, with the Act for the Reconstruction of the State, the power of the *Länder* was removed completely. Germany was no longer seen as a country of different regions but as a highly centralised state. The states were reduced to mere provinces split into 42 *Gaue*, each run by a *Gauleiter* directly elected by the party and answerable to central government.

The People's Court

Hitler had been infuriated by the trial of those accused of causing the Reichstag Fire. Four Communists had been acquitted with just one, Van der Lubbe, being sentenced to death. So, in April 1934, the Nazis passed the Act to Set Up the People's Court. This created a separate court outside the normal justice system. It dealt with 'political offences' and ensured rapid decisions. 'Political offences' was a deliberately vague term and those tried in these courts ranged from slow workers to treason plotters. The number of death penalties that they issued rose rapidly as the years passed.

▼ Judge Friesler opening the proceedings at a people's court, c.1934

Record

Complete your seventh card. Use the title 'Further legislation (July 1933 to August 1934)'. On one side, summarise the two laws described above and, on the other, explain why these laws increased the Nazis' hold on Germany.

The Night of the Long Knives

By 1934, two potential threats to Hitler's power remained.

One threat came from the non-Nazi Conservatives who had been given places in the cabinet when Hitler was made Chancellor. Their leader was the Vice-Chancellor, Franz von Papen. Rumours were circulating that he planned to take Hitler's place.

The second threat came from Hitler's own stormtroopers, the SA. By 1934, the SA was becoming increasingly violent and difficult to control. It was growing rapidly: by the beginning of 1934 it had six times as many men as at the start of 1933 and numbered nearly three million.

What made the SA a particularly significant threat was the leadership of Ernst Röhm. He had openly declared that he wanted the SA to take over the army. Hitler, however, could see that although the army had only 100,000 men and was dwarfed by the SA, it was better equipped and easier to control. Hitler rejected Röhm's takeover plans. Röhm was indignant and began openly criticising Hitler, whom he referred to as the 'ridiculous corporal' in front of his men. There is no evidence, however, that he was actively plotting Hitler's downfall.

Deadly attacks

Hitler needed to do something about these two threats before they endangered his power. He dealt with both in June of 1934. First, he tasked the SS to begin manufacturing evidence that Röhm was planning a nationwide uprising. Next, lists were drawn up of 'politically unreliable' people. Naturally these included Röhm and other SA leaders, as well as von Papen and other political rivals. On 30 June, in what would become known as the Night of the Long Knives, the SS went into swift and decisive action against these carefully identified enemies.

The SA leaders, including Röhm, had been instructed to go to a hotel outside Munich for a special meeting. There was no meeting. Along with SS officers, Hitler, Goebbels and others entered the hotel, arrested the SA leadership and sent them to prison, where many were killed. Röhm was given the option to commit suicide but refused. Just two days after his arrest, he was brutally murdered by two SS officers.

Beyond the SA

In Berlin, Göring was in charge of the operation. He did not stop with the SA and moved on to the Conservatives. Von Papen escaped arrest as he was too prominent a figure. After an interview with Hitler, though, he resigned from office. His secretary and leading supporters were arrested. Hitler used the opportunity to get rid of other older enemies too. Von Schleicher (the previous Chancellor), von Kahr (who had thwarted their attempt to take power in 1923) and Erich Klausener (a prominent Catholic) were killed. In total at least 85 people, 12 of whom were prominent Reichstag deputies, were murdered. The 'long knives' had devastating effects.

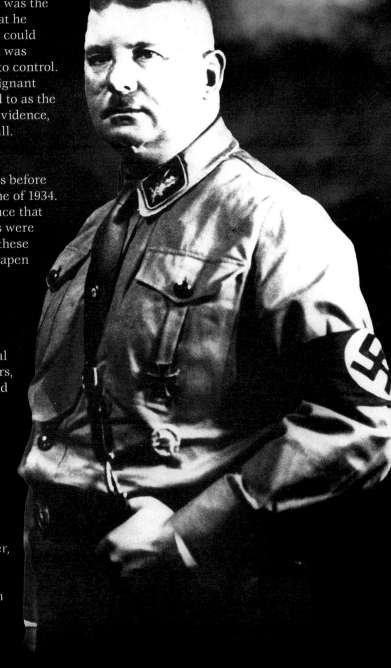

▲ Ernst Röhm, leader of the SA, c.1932

The consequences of the Night of the Long Knives

In the days after the Night of the Long Knives, Hitler used the radio and other media to assure everyone in Germany and beyond that all was under control, and that the deaths and arrests had been for the good of Germany. Historians can now see how they actually accelerated Hitler's move towards total control of German life through consequences such as those shown in the chart below.

Soon after the Night of the Long Knives, one retired army officer saw that many generals and other serving soldiers were expressing their joy at the fall of the SA. He told them:

> If you look on without lifting a finger, you will meet the same fate sooner or later.

Reflect

Does the comment made by the retired officer (see left) support the view that the Night of the Long Knives created a culture of fear?

The power of the SA was reduced:
The Night of the Long Knives certainly curbed the power of the SA. Its leaders now knew the consequences of questioning Hitler. The role of the SA was reduced, although it continued to exist. Its membership dropped severely from 2.9 million in August 1934 to 1.6 million by October 1935.

The Nazi regime gained a strange legal grounding:
The Night of the Long Knives involved the execution without trial of at least 85 people. In a speech to the Reichstag on 13 July 1934, Hitler insisted that he was the 'supreme judge of the German people'. He had established that 'extra judicial' killing by the regime was acceptable.

Consequences of the Night of the Long Knives

(30 June 1934)

The loyalty of the army was secured:
The army (the *Reichswehr*) knew that Hitler had made a choice between them and the SA. When he chose to give his support to the army they repaid him with great loyalty. General Blomberg, the head of the *Reichswehr*, congratulated Hitler on his 'soldierly decision' to deal with the 'traitors and murderers'.

A culture of fear was created:
The SS, not the SA, now became the key instrument of Nazi terror in the German state. The culture of fear that followed the Night of the Long Knives was by far its most important consequence.

The rise of the SS and Heinrich Himmler was established:
The success of the Night of the Long Knives was largely down to the SS and Heinrich Himmler who had co-ordinated it. Himmler's men were crucial in the operation, leading the arrests and murdering the opponents. Before this, the SS had been a relatively small off-shoot of the SA. They had now proven their loyalty, and rose in prominence. Himmler would go on to become one of the most powerful men in Germany.

Record

Use the information on pages 21–22 to write a card about 'The Night of the Long Knives (June and July 1934)'. On one side, summarise the main events. On the other, explain how the consequences helped the Nazis to increase their control.

Becoming the *Führer*

There was now just one final obstacle to Hitler assuming full power: President Hindenburg. Although Hitler was Chancellor and had the power to make laws, the German constitution allowed the president to block any action by a chancellor. However, by late July it was clear that President Hindenburg would not be an obstacle for much longer: the 87 year old was dying. On 1 August, Hitler visited the President who, in his deluded state, referred to him as 'Your Majesty'. Hindenburg was at death's door. Hitler and the Nazis worked quickly to pass legislation and seize the moment.

Later that day, the Act concerning the Head of State was passed. At the moment of Hindenburg's death, the office and power of the President would be merged with that of the Chancellor under the new title of *Führer*. That moment came a day later, at 9 a.m. on 2 August 1934.

Hitler was now *Führer*, literally meaning 'leader'. He was the dictator of Germany, with full power, a position he would hold until he committed suicide in April 1945.

▼ President Hindenburg on his deathbed, August 1934

◀ Adolf Hitler delivering one of his first speeches as *Führer*, August 1934

Record

Complete your final card. Use the title 'Becoming the *Führer* (August 1934)'. On one side, summarise the events around the death of Hindenburg. On the other, explain why these events gave Hitler total control over Germany.

Review

By now you should have nine 'Nazi control cards' and a good understanding of how Hitler and the Nazis took control of Germany. Use them to reinforce your knowledge and deepen your understanding. You could:

a) Place the cards 'summary side up'. Test how many of the explanations about the Nazis' increasing power you can remember.
b) Place the cards 'explanation side up' and see how well you can remember the relevant events and dates on the summary side.
c) Place the cards along a timeline in chronological (date) order. Leave short gaps between events that came close together in time and wider gaps for events that were separated by longer periods of time. What do you notice about the pace of change?
d) Keep the cards in chronological order. Move them up or down depending on how significant each one was in helping the Nazis take control of Germany between 1933 and 1934.

23

The 'dark charisma' of Adolf Hitler

Laurence Rees is a British historian who specialises in the history of Nazi Germany and the Second World War. In 2012, he produced a BBC TV documentary about Adolf Hitler and wrote a book to accompany the series. Rees wanted to understand why so many people in Germany followed Hitler. He pointed out that, in many ways, Hitler's personality made his popularity unlikely:

> Adolf Hitler was, at first sight, the most unlikely leader of a sophisticated state at the heart of Europe. He was incapable of normal human friendships, unable to debate intellectually, filled with hatred and prejudice, bereft of any real capacity to love …

But alongside these negative aspects of his personality, Hitler possessed great powers of persuasion. Many of the people whom Rees interviewed spoke of Hitler's 'charisma':

> When pressed on the reason why they found such a strange figure so persuasive they pointed to a myriad of factors, like the circumstances of the time, their fears, their hopes and so on. But many also described the powerful sense of attraction they felt for Hitler – something that a number of people ascribed to his 'charisma'.

Hitler had a remarkable ability to connect with an audience. People who met him often commented on the intensity of his gaze. Those who heard his speeches were often inspired by his certainty about Germany's destiny and by his emotional intensity. Rees explained:

> The ability to feel events emotionally and to demonstrate that emotion to others was a crucial part of his charismatic appeal.

But, in the end, Hitler's charismatic leadership, and his popularity with many German people, allowed him to do terrible things. Hitler's charisma was a 'dark charisma'. Laurence Rees believes that there is a warning in this for our lives today:

> … only by understanding how those who seek power try to influence us, and how we often actively participate in our own manipulation, can we finally understand the dangers we face if we leave rationality and scepticism aside and, instead, put our faith in a leader with charisma.

All quotations are from Laurence Rees's book, *The Dark Charisma of Adolf Hitler: Leading Millions into the Abyss*, published in 2012.

▲ Adolf Hitler, c.1933

Reflect

How do the photographs on the page opposite support Laurence Rees's view that Hitler was a charismatic leader?

◄ Hitler and SA troops at the Brown House, Munich, c.1930

► Hitler giving a speech during the election campaign for the Reich's Presidency, Berlin, 1932

◄ Hitler meeting workers at the Siemens factory, Berlin, 10 November 1933

Taking a stand

What made it so hard to oppose Nazi rule?

▼ A crowd celebrating the launch of a German ship in 1936

The Enquiry

In 1933, only 33 per cent of the population had voted for the Nazis and yet three years later it appeared that support was widespread. This photograph was taken in 1936, at the launch of a new navy ship in Hamburg. The crowd stands with outstretched arms saluting their *Führer* with the *Hitlergrüsse* (Hitler greeting).

The Nazis spent a lot of time and effort to win this sort of response from the German people. At first sight, the image suggests that they had established the total control that they wanted. But look again. To the right and top of the crowd, one man stands with his arms defiantly folded in protest. This man is August Landmesser. Until 1935, Landmesser had been a Nazi but was expelled from the party when its new laws stopped him from marrying the love of his life, Irma Eckler, who was Jewish. From that day, Landmesser

openly defied the Nazis. He and Irma lived together and had two children before she was murdered in a death camp in 1942. August Landmesser was killed in action in 1944 after being forced to fight in the German army.

In this enquiry you will build up a bigger picture about three aspects of Nazi rule, 1933–39:

● how the Nazis controlled the people through **fear**
● how the Nazis tried to win the hearts and minds of the German people through **propaganda**
● the extent to which there was **opposition** to the Nazi regime from the people in Germany.

At the end you will explain why it was so hard to oppose Nazi rule in Germany and how typical was the opposition of people like August Landmesser.

The machinery of terror

The main method of Nazi control was through its machinery of terror, a complex system of intimidation, intelligence gathering and policing. The point of this was to remove any element of direct opposition to Nazi rule and leave the rest of the population in such a state of fear that they felt compelled to blindly follow the Nazi rules.

Record

In the centre of an A3 sheet of paper, make a simple copy of the image shown here. Leave lots of space around the edges. At the top, write the heading **'The Nazi machinery of terror'**.

As you work through pages 27 to 31 surround the image with notes about each part of the Nazi 'machinery of terror' that you learn about. Be sure to summarise what each part of the Nazi machine of terror did and how it kept people in fear.

Start by using the information below to summarise what you have learned about the man at the centre of the machinery of terror: Heinrich Himmler.

Himmler and the SS

Heinrich Himmler was born in Munich to a middle-class family and joined the Nazis in 1923. He became a member of the SS (*Schutzstaffel*), an off-shoot group of the SA with around 250 members whose job was to provide a bodyguard for Hitler. In 1929, Himmler was made leader (*Reichsführer*) of the SS and he began transforming this tiny group into an elite paramilitary force.

Its members, who wore special black uniforms with the SS double lightning bolt logo, had a reputation for blind obedience and total commitment. Unlike the SA, the SS was kept small. By 1933, it still had only 52,000 members, compared with 3 million in the SA. Himmler was ruthless about selection, focusing on men of pure German blood who had the ideal Aryan features (see page 54).

It was in 1934 that the SS truly rose to power. On the Night of the Long Knives (see page 21) the dominance of the SA was removed and from that point Hitler looked to the obedience and ruthlessness of the SS to carry out purges, removing his enemies. The SS was made an independent organisation and over the next few years Himmler absorbed more and more of the policing power over Germany. In 1936, he became *Reichsführer* and Chief of all German Police, which made him one of the most powerful men in Nazi Germany.

Himmler once summed up his views by saying:

> The best political weapon is the weapon of terror. Cruelty commands respect. Men may hate us. But we don't ask for their love; only for their fear.

▼ Heinrich Himmler, c.1934

Reflect

Why do think Himmler wanted to be Chief of Police as well as head of the SS?

Intelligence gathering

In order to control the German people, the Nazis monitored them closely through an elaborate intelligence-gathering system.

The SD

The SD (*Sicherheitsdienst* or Secret Service in English) was the main official intelligence-gathering agency. Originally set up to serve the Nazi Party, it developed under its sinister leader, Reinhard Heydrich, and became the state Secret Service in 1938.

The role of the SD was to identify actual or potential enemies of the Nazi leadership. It had a few hundred full-time agents and several thousand volunteer informants. Historians investigating the SD have found that most SD agents were relatively young, well-educated men who showed no sign of being fanatical Nazis.

The SD focused on any opposition to the party itself. It spied on all aspects of education, the arts, government and administration, as well as churches and the Jewish community. It also tracked foreign reporting of German affairs and looked out for spy networks serving other nations.

From their findings, agents wrote extensive reports on the morale and attitude of the German people. These enabled the Nazi leadership to monitor the impact of the changes they made and to tailor propaganda as and when it was necessary. The SD did not take action against individuals but passed information on to those who did – the Gestapo.

Reinhard Heydrich

The leader of the SD was Reinhard Heydrich. This photograph of him sharing time with his wife and sons on a beach may suggest that he was a kind and homely figure but nothing could be further from the truth. Hitler once described Heydrich as 'the man with the iron heart'.

Heydrich joined the SS in 1931 and made such an impression on the Nazi leadership that he was asked to lead the new SD the following year. By 1934, he was also head of the Gestapo. This put him at the epicentre of the Nazi regime and his fingerprints can be seen on nearly every notable and horrific event committed by that regime in the following decade. In 1934, it was his Gestapo team that built a dossier of evidence against Röhm and carried out many of the murders during the Night of the Long Knives.

In June 1936, when all the police forces of Germany were united into a single force, Himmler became its director, with Heydrich as his deputy. From this point, they were the two most important people in controlling the German nation.

▲ Reinhard Heydrich on the beach with his family, c.1935

Reflect

What made Reinhard Heydrich such a powerful man in Germany by 1936?

The Gestapo

The Gestapo (Secret Police) was undoubtedly the most infamous organisation within the Nazi terror system. Similar to the SD, the Gestapo spied on the public to remove any opposition. Whereas the SD was originally a Nazi organisation, the Gestapo began as the Prussian state police and was expanded into a nationwide group, not directly controlled by the party itself. Göring, its original leader, said its task was 'to investigate all political activities in the entire state that pose a danger to the state'. This explains why it made sense to put the Gestapo alongside the SD, under the control of Heydrich in 1936.

At its height, the Gestapo had 15,000 active officers to police a population of 66 million. This works out as only one officer per 4,400 people. Yet even with such low numbers, the Gestapo was deeply feared. It was a highly effective, ruthless organisation that had the power to arrest and imprison any person suspected of opposing the Nazi state.

In the early years after 1933, the Gestapo focused on the Nazis' political opponents but, later on, Jews, homosexuals and religious dissenters were also targeted.

It was the Gestapo's ability to identify opponents that gave them such frightening power. They could tap telephones and open mail, but mostly they relied on informers who might pass on remarks they had overheard or just general suspicions. A lot of useful information came from the Nazi party's system of Block Leaders that had originally been set up to spread the Nazi message. The Block Leaders were men who were given the job of getting to know the people living in the 40 to 60 residences in their local area. This extract from an article in a Nazi magazine written in 1934 explains what the Block Leader (or Warden) should aim to do:

> The Block warden knows very well all the party members and non-party members in his district. He must know about their families and jobs, as well as all other personal relationships. He must know their concerns, whether large or small. He must know their political and social opinions … Showing friendliness and concern to both party members and non-party members, sharing and understanding their joys and sorrows, must and will help to win the confidence of our people's comrades such that in time they come to see the cell or block leader as a kind of political pastor (priest).

Other tip offs (or 'denunciations') came from the general public. All denunciations, no matter how trivial, were investigated and the accused were brought into Gestapo offices for interrogation. Quite often the Gestapo discovered that a tip-off was based on a grudge. For example, one housewife in Mannheim told the Gestapo her husband was always criticising the Nazis. When they investigated the case, it emerged that the wife wanted her husband to be taken away so that she could continue a love affair she was having with a soldier.

The aim of interrogation was to get the accused to confess. Memoirs of survivors tell us that torture, such as beatings with rubber truncheons or bamboo canes, sleep deprivation and electrocution, was sometimes used. The extent of this is difficult to evaluate as the Gestapo destroyed almost all its papers in the final days of the war. Only three sets of records remain, from Speyer, Wurzburg and Düsseldorf. These reveal the sources that led to each person's arrest. This chart shows what these were in a batch of 825 arrests made in Düsseldorf in 1933–34:

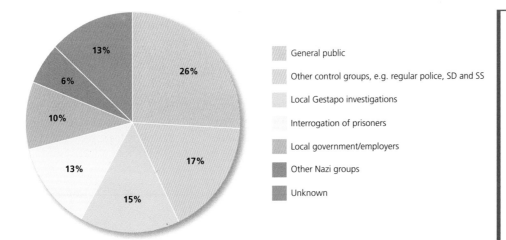

General public — 26%

Other control groups, e.g. regular police, SD and SS

Local Gestapo investigations

Interrogation of prisoners

Local government/employers

Other Nazi groups

Unknown

▲ Sources leading to arrests in Düsseldorf, 1933–34

Reflect

In his book *The Gestapo*, 2015, the historian Frank McDonough has written that:

> Nazi propaganda liked to give the impression that Gestapo officers were everywhere. Nothing could be further from the truth.

How useful are the extract from the 1934 article about Block Leaders, the data in the pie chart and this statement by Frank McDonough, for a historian studying the Gestapo?

The police, judges and courts

When the Nazis took control of Germany they inherited a justice system that had professional and independent police and judges. They did not abolish this but sought to modify and control it. Any potential enemies were removed from their ranks and Nazis were moved into leadership positions. Controlling the justice system meant that the Nazis could fully enforce any new laws they passed and issue whatever punishments they wanted against those found guilty.

Police

Many police reacted positively to Nazi rule as their powers were extended. The Nazis centralised police organisations and provided them with far better funding. In 1936, the police were put under the control of the SS and were encouraged to join its forces. The Orpo (ordinary police) and Kripo (criminal police) continued to carry out their everyday duties in the community and investigated crimes, as they had done before the Nazi takeover of power, but they also became an important part of the terror system, providing intelligence on potential enemies and arresting them.

▲ Members of police forces run a race in full uniform to show their fitness at a Nazi rally, 1937

Judges and courts

Judges had to swear an oath to Hitler, and sentences during the Nazi era became more severe. The number of criminal offences punishable by a death sentence rose from 3 in 1933 to 46 in 1943; 40,000 people were sent to their deaths. Many of these death sentences were given by the People's Court (see page 20) where the lack of a jury and predetermined guilty verdicts meant the proceedings were no more than show trials.

In 1936, Professor Karl Eckhardt, a Nazi legal expert summed up the system of justice in Germany at that time:

> The judge is to safeguard the order of the racial community, to prosecute all acts harmful to the community and to arbitrate in disagreements. The National Socialist ideology, especially as expressed in the party programme and in the speeches of our Führer, is the basis for interpreting legal sources.

Reflect

Which development do you think would have frightened the German people more: the ending of trial by jury or the control of the police by the SS?

◀ A judge swearing loyalty to Hitler, 1936

Concentration camps

Other than execution, the ultimate punishment for those hunted down by the terror system was the concentration camp. Unlike the extermination camps, such as Auschwitz, whose primary purpose was killing people, these concentration camps aimed to gather people who threatened the state and to 'concentrate' them in places where they could be kept away from society and in harsh conditions.

The early years

Over 70 concentration camps were set up in 1933 to imprison 45,000 Communists, trades unionists and other political opponents. These early 'wild' camps gave out extreme punishments, to the extent that some guards were jailed for torturing prisoners. Many were run by the SA, and these were so disorganised and had such extreme conditions that they became an embarrassment and were closed in the second half of 1933. Most prisoners were freed at that point and the total number of prisoners dropped to 7500.

Later years and 'Death's Head' units

In June 1933, Theodor Eicke was appointed to run Dachau and bring order to the chaos. His Death's Head units, guards who wore skulls on their SS hats, established a code of conduct that was used in all the camps, with specific punishments for different offences. Lesser offences could result in a diet of only bread and water, while greater ones could result in flogging or beatings carried out in front of other prisoners. In 1937, Himmler declared that guards could not be sent to jail for their actions and deaths went up dramatically at the camps. At Dachau there were 69 deaths in 1937, nearly seven times as many as in the previous year. During the same period, the camps also began using the prisoners for labour, forcing them to carry out manual work in and out of the camps.

In the early years, the camps mostly imprisoned political opponents but, by the mid-1930s, other groups began to arrive – criminals, the work shy, religious opponents and to a lesser extent Jews. In 1938, at Buchenwald, 4600 of the 8000 inmates were 'work shy'. Camp authorities imposed a uniform on the imprisoned, and different groups were forced to wear different-coloured triangles. By the start of the war, the total number of prisoners had risen again to 21,000.

▲ Dachau, Germany, 1938. Inmates at a roll-call

Reflect

Why might the Nazis have been embarrassed by the early camps but not by what they became later on?

Record

Complete the diagram as described on page 27. Add a paragraph explaining why this 'Machinery of Terror' worked so well.

The range and effectiveness of Nazi propaganda

Fear is not enough to control a population. In order for the Nazis to strengthen their control over the German people, they also needed to win their hearts and minds. On 13 March 1933, the Ministry of Public Enlightenment and Propaganda was created. The man in charge was Joseph Goebbels, a highly intelligent and driven Nazi, who established a wide range of propaganda designed to spread the Nazi message and crush any dissenting views.

Record

On a second A3 sheet of paper, make a new notes diagram with a simple copy of this sketch of Joseph Goebbels at the centre. Use the heading '**Nazi propaganda**'. Surround the image with notes on pages 32–36. Describe each form of propaganda that you have read about and explain its impact.

▲ Joseph Goebbels, c.1934

Newspapers

The Nazis controlled newspapers through the Reich Press Chamber in two ways.

1   They took control of existing papers and closed any opposition papers down. By 1939, they owned two-thirds of all German newspapers and magazines. The Nazis even published their own party newspapers, including the sensationalist *Der Stürmer* (The Stormer). This printed anti-Semitic rants and cartoons like the one shown on this page where a Jew is depicted crucifying Jesus.

2   The Nazis controlled the content of newspapers. The Editor's Law meant editors were personally responsible for content and were not allowed to print anything 'which is calculated to weaken the strength of the German Reich at home or abroad'. All journalists were forced to join the Reich Association of the Press and Goebbels issued regular statements about what could and could not be printed.

▶ A copy of *Der Stürmer* from 1937. The headline reads 'Judaism against Christianity'. The article and the image encourage Germans to see Jews as enemies of Christians.

Radio

In the days before television, radio was the best way to get a message across to the masses. In 1934, all national and local radio stations across Germany were incorporated into the Reich Radio Company, and the Ministry of Propaganda controlled its output. Goebbels said that the first law of broadcast should be 'Don't be boring!' but most producers played it safe and played Nazi speeches along with traditional German folk music or Hitler's favourite composer, Wagner. American culture like jazz music was discouraged, as was music by Jewish composers and songwriters.

The Nazis produced cheap radio sets, the People's Receivers. These were sold at a week's wage for the average manual worker and could be paid for in instalments. In 1933, 1.5 million of these sets were produced, and by 1939, 70 per cent of Germans had a radio in their home, the highest percentage of any country in the world. To aid control, the People's Receiver had a very limited range, which meant that they were not powerful enough to pick up foreign stations.

▶ A 'People's Receiver'

Rallies

Giant rallies were held to emphasise and celebrate the strength of the Nazi movement. They involved speeches, choruses, marches, torch-lit parades and even mock battles. The annual party rally at Nuremberg was the largest of these and the 1934 event lasted a whole week. (That is where the image on pages 8–9 was taken.)

For that 1934 rally, 500 trains carried 250,000 people to a specially built railway station from where they went to stay in a city of tents constructed for the event. A total of 30,000 swastika flags were placed around the field, each with its own spotlight. At night, 152 searchlights projected beams of light into the sky, producing what the Nazis called the 'cathedral of light'.

The whole event was filmed by Leni Riefenstahl, a remarkable woman with great creative gifts. Her film, *Triumph of the Will*, opened with shots of Hitler's aeroplane descending from the skies over Nuremberg, bringing him to Earth like a god. At the time, many of the crowd were moved by this semi-religious atmosphere and became hysterical when the *Führer* made his appearances.

◀ Leni Riefenstahl's camera crews filming the Nuremberg Rally, 1934

Reflect

Why do you think Hitler and Goebbels asked Leni Riefenstahl to make *Triumph of the Will*?

Posters

The Nazis were masters of the visual message. Propaganda posters were put up around towns and villages across Germany throughout their years in power. The pictures on this selection of posters make the messages clear and obvious, even to those with no knowledge of the German language ... but the key words are translated below each one.

Reflect

Look at each of the posters in turn.

1. What is the effect of the image and words on each one? (The key words are translated under each.)
2. What overall themes emerge from these posters?
3. How effective do you think these posters might have been?

Long live Germany!

Hitler is building (the nation) – help by buying German goods

The NSDP (Nazi Party) safeguards the people of the nation

Our GERMAN railways

The German student fights for the *Führer* and the people

Then and now, we remain comrades, The German Workers Front

35

Berlin Olympics

In 1936, the Olympic Games were held in Berlin and were used as an important piece of Nazi propaganda. Olympic flags and swastikas covered Berlin, including the new 100,000-seat stadium, one of the biggest in the world at the time. Anti-Semitic signs were taken down and German newspapers toned down their stories to give the impression of a Germany that was acceptable internationally.

However, the Games promoted Aryan superiority and the nearly all-Aryan German team emerged victorious, winning the most medals. There were notable exceptions though: Luz Long was the ultimate Aryan hero – a blond-haired, blue-eyed German long jumper. Long broke the Olympic record in the preliminary round, whereas his opponent Jesse Owens, an African American who was far from the Nazi Aryan ideal, fouled his first two attempts. Long, being sportsmanlike, gave Owens advice about where to jump from and Owens went on to get the gold. Long ended up with silver.

▶ Carl Ludwig 'Luz' Long, winning silver in the long-jump event, 4 August 1936

Film

The 1930s were the golden age of cinema and in Germany this was no different. As they did with other media, the Nazis closely controlled films through a new organisation, the Reich Film Chamber. Complicated laws and taxes limited the import of foreign films and money was provided to make home-grown German films. By 1939, two-thirds of all films made were state financed.

In 1934, the Reich Cinema Law made it compulsory that all scripts had to be pre-censored, which stopped production of any films that criticised the Nazis. Films that glorified the leader or criticised the Jews were encouraged but Goebbels realised that overly political films would not be popular so limited this to only 10 per cent of films made.

Films such as the one advertised by this poster were not openly filled with propaganda but blended romance and drama with themes that matched Nazi beliefs. In this case, a German pilot is shot down over France during the First World War and is rescued by a young French woman. It explores his duty in this situation and is called *Patriots*.

▶ Poster for the film *Patrioten*, 1937

Record

Complete the diagram as described on page 32. Add a paragraph explaining why Nazi propaganda worked so well.

Opposition to Nazi rule, including the Left, Church leaders and youth groups

Record

By now you should know how the Nazis tightened their grip on the German people through terror and propaganda. On the whole, their approach was extremely successful, but it would be wrong to think that everyone obediently followed the Nazis. Some Germans resisted their grip and provided opposition.

On a third A3 sheet of paper, make a new notes diagram with a simple copy of this sketch of August Landmesser at the centre. Use the heading '**Opposition to Nazi rule**'. Surround the image with notes on pages 37–41. For each person or group, summarise how and why they took a stand against the Nazis and what happened to them.

The Left

In the early years of the Third Reich, the most active and persistent opposition came from the two left-wing political parties that rejected the right-wing ideology of the Nazis: the Social Democrats and Communists.

The Social Democrats

After the Nazi take-over in 1933, the leaders of the Social Democrats, who were more moderate than the Communists, fled the country. This left those who remained in Germany without clear leadership, but they still formed small resistance groups. One of the largest, in Hanover, had just 250 members.

These groups worked secretly in the industrial areas of Germany. They produced anti-Nazi leaflets and posters, but were hunted down by the Gestapo, who arrested 1200 of them in the Rhine Ruhr region alone.

If the Social Democrats had combined forces with the Communists, they might have provided a serious opposition to the Nazis, but the long-standing rivalries between the two groups limited their effectiveness.

The Communists

The Communists were more active than the Social Democrats. They aimed to provide visible resistance with meetings, propaganda and newsletters. One of these newsletters, *The Red Flag*, produced 10,000 copies at least once a month. However, this visibility meant Communists were easily identified and soon arrested by the Gestapo.

One Communist and trade unionist, a carpenter called Georg Esler, was so appalled at the conditions of German workers and so fearful of a war that he attempted to kill Hitler in 1939. Working entirely on his own, Esler planted a time-bomb in a hall where Hitler was due to give a speech. Purely by luck, Hitler left the room thirteen minutes before the bomb exploded. Esler was caught, locked in Dachau for five years and then executed.

After studying all the different groups that dared to oppose the Nazis, the historian Richard J. Evans reached this interpretation:

> Of all the groups who held out against Nazism in the early years of the Third Reich, the Communists were the most persistent and the most undaunted. They paid the greatest price as a consequence.

Reflect

In 2015, a German director made a film called *Thirteen Minutes*. It told the story of Georg Esler's plot.

What reasons might he have had for making this film?

The Church

With about 22 million Catholics, 40 million Protestants and some other smaller denominations, religious groups were by far the largest non-Nazi organisations in Germany. With their teachings and beliefs about love and forgiveness, it is unsurprising that there was opposition to the Nazis from the Church.

Hitler saw this as a potential threat and put measures in place to control the Church:

- In July 1933, he made an agreement called the 'Concordat' with the leader of the Catholic Church, Pope Pius XI. The Pope promised that German Catholics would stay out of politics if, in return, the Nazis would leave them alone.
- With the Protestants, a new Reich Church was set up in which the pastors had to swear an oath to Hitler.

Despite his promises, Hitler interfered with both churches. In 1936, all Church youth groups were stopped. By 1939, nearly all Church schools had been closed, and arrests of priests who spoke out against the Nazis began to increase, which in turn led to more resistance.

▼ A Nazi procession outside a church at Gutwasser in 1938. It marked the funeral of a local Nazi Party member.

Often resistance from pastors was limited to protecting their own institutions but some went further and criticised the Nazi regime, in particular in relation to its treatment of the Jews.

Martin Niemöller

First World War hero Martin Niemöller, a Protestant pastor, became one of the most prominent critics of the Nazis. Refusing to join the Reich Church, Niemöller founded an alternative, the non-Nazi Confessional Church. By 1934, 6000 pastors had joined, leaving only 2000 in the Reich Church. Niemöller and the Confessional Church preached against Nazi racial policy, and over 800 pastors were arrested and sent to concentration camps. Niemöller was sent to Sachsenhausen and then Dachau, but survived the ordeal.

Paul Schneider

Schneider was the first priest to be murdered by the Nazis. A small-town Protestant pastor, he began to preach against Nazi Church policy in 1933. After joining Niemöller's Confessional Church, he was arrested in 1934 and again in 1935. He was warned to stop his protest but continued regardless. In 1937, he even banned parishioners who were Nazi Party members from attending his church services. Following their complaints, he was imprisoned at Buchenwald concentration camp, where he was murdered by lethal injection in 1939.

Pope Pius XI

Although it had been Pope Pius who signed the 1933 Concordat with the Nazis, by 1937 he had had enough. He wrote a letter called 'With Burning Anxiety' which was smuggled in to Germany and read out in all Catholic churches on Palm Sunday. (This was always one of the biggest congregations of the year.) The letter condemned Nazi beliefs and methods. The next day the Gestapo raided every Catholic church, seizing all copies of the letter. In the following months, the Nazis intensified their actions against the Church.

Cardinal Galen

As the Catholic Bishop of Münster, Galen initially welcomed the Nazis. At his consecration as Bishop in 1933 there were stormtroopers and swastika flags. But, by 1934, his sermons began to criticise the Nazi regime over its racial policy. The Gestapo were sent to question Galen, but he was too high profile to remove from power or persecute, so he continued to provide resistance.

Jehovah's Witnesses

Due to the rules of their faith, Jehovah's Witnesses were unwilling to comply with the Nazi state. They refused to give the Hitler salute and, following their pacifist beliefs, refused compulsory military service. Both outside and within Germany, they began writing anti-Nazi leaflets. As a result, the Gestapo created a special unit to combat the Witnesses and, by 1939, 6000 were imprisoned in concentration camps.

▶ The Kusserow family in a photograph taken c.1935. They were all Jehovah's Witnesses. Every one of them was arrested in 1936 and most were held in concentration camps until the end of the war in 1945.

Youth groups

Young people are often idealistic and question authority. This was no different in Nazi Germany, and in the years 1933–39 young people provided some of the most significant opposition to the regime. They opposed the Nazis for a wide range of reasons:

- **Politics** – some did not agree with the way the country was being run.
- **Religion** – some were angry at the way their religion was being treated by the Nazis.
- **Culture** – some were frustrated at the enforced youth groups and disbanding of traditional youth organisations.

There was not a nationwide movement of youth resistance, but local groups formed in various regions of Germany. None of these posed a particular threat to the Nazis, but they all resisted the pressure to conform to the Nazi ideal.

You can read about four of the main groups here:

Young Communists

The Communist Youth Federation of Germany, like its adult counterpart, was banned in Germany, but the young Communists continued to meet in secret. They disguised their meetings as unpolitical activities such as hikes in the countryside. In Leipzig, 1500 young people joined *meuten* or gangs. There were at least twenty gangs, most of which were Communist. They dressed differently, in short leather trousers, checked shirts and bright neck scarves. Some wrote anti-Nazi flyers.

Christians

In 1933, there were 2.5 million members of Christian youth organisations in Germany. All of these were banned as the Nazis only wanted people to be part of the official Hitler Youth groups. Many Christians met anyway in resistance to this and some went on illegal pilgrimages.

Swing Kids

These young people came together to listen to jazz, dance and talk openly. Swing, a style of music associated with African Americans, was banned by the Nazis. The Swing Kids wanted to develop their own individual personalities. In contrast to the Nazi ideal, they had long hair and wore special clothes, like the wide trousers you can see in the photo below. Himmler saw the group as so dangerous he personally wrote to Heydrich, asking the Gestapo to deal with them. Many were arrested and some were sent to concentration camps.

Reflect

Lots of these opposition figures are honoured in modern-day Germany. The Swing Kids' story was even made into a big Hollywood film. Why would people want to honour people who posed little threat to the Nazis?

▲ Swing Kids in Hamburg in 1941

Edelweiss Pirates

Formed in the Rhine Ruhr region in around 1938, all members of this group wore an Edelweiss flower or a white pin on their clothing. They went on excursions, organised camps and sang songs. Some listened to foreign radio and spread news. They produced flyers and painted slogans on walls. Some actively picked fights with the Nazis, with reported beatings of the Hitler Youth members. Bartholomäus Schink (pictured here) was arrested for being in the group and was publicly hanged in 1944.

An Edelweiss Pirates song

Hitler's dictates make us small,
we're yet bound in chains.
But one day we'll again walk tall,
no chain can us restrain.
For hard are our fists,
Yes! And knives at our wrists,
for youth to be free.

Reflect

What can this song tell us about the Pirates' motives and actions?

▲ Bartholomäus Schink, a member the Edelweiss Pirates, c.1944

Record

Use the information on pages 37–41 to complete the diagram as described on page 37.

Review

In this enquiry you have produced three diagrams that give the bigger picture of three issues:

- how the Nazis controlled people through **fear**
- how the Nazis controlled people through **propaganda**
- how much **opposition** there was to Nazi ideas and laws.

Your challenge now is to combine these into a single coherent answer.

Imagine that a friend has said to you that he or she is surprised that there was so very little opposition to Nazi rule in Germany between 1933 and 1939. Write down what you would say in response. Remember to include fear, propaganda and opposition in your answer.

Scared of sunflowers

▶ '*Reife Sonnenblumen* (Ripe Sunflowers)', painted by Emil Nolde, c.1932

This painting is called '*Reife Sonnenblumen* (Ripe Sunflowers)' and at first glance it appears very innocent; a pleasing oil painting of some bright flowers. Yet the Nazis believed this painting was 'degenerate'. This meant that they thought it was abnormal, immoral and corrupt. The story of this painting and the artist who created it, Emil Nolde, reveals the extent to which the Nazis controlled Germany and their paranoia about those elements of society that were deemed un-German.

The party member

▼ Emil Nolde, c.1930

Emil Nolde was born in 1867 and by the 1920s had become quite a famous artist in Germany. Using oil paint with bold colours, he had an 'expressionist' style that looked similar to that of Vincent van Gogh, whom he admired. Nolde moved all over Germany, but by the 1920s had settled his studio in Berlin. Lots of his work was of flowers, like the painting here, but many paintings demonstrated his Christianity and used biblical stories as their inspiration, while others reflected the vibrancy of nightlife in the 1920s.

Nolde was a patriotic German with nationalistic views. There is also evidence that he was anti-Semitic, writing deeply unpleasant critiques to Jewish artists. Given these views, it is unsurprising that in the early 1920s Nolde joined the Nazi Party. In 1932, at the height of his fame, Nolde painted '*Reife Sonnenblumen*' and in 1933 was made President of the State Academy of Arts in Berlin.

The party reject

By 1936 things had changed dramatically. Since their rise to power in 1933, the Nazis had been taking control of the media, removing any element that was considered un-German. Art did not escape this. Joseph Goebbel's propaganda ministry began removing any art from museums that did not fit with Nazi ideology or that they considered to be Jewish or communist in nature. In essence this meant anything modern, abstract or unusual. Nolde, the committed Nazi Party member and supporter, was not exempt. In 1936, he was told to cease artistic activity and, in 1937, a total of 1052 of his paintings were removed from German museums, more than any other artist. Nolde's work was considered to be too modern and offensive. 'Reife Sonnenblumen' was one of these paintings.

Looking at the painting now it really is very difficult to see how this work could ever be considered offensive. But the Nazi authorities were keen that art should only contain images that promoted their ideas and were scared that different art, like these sunflowers, would have a negative impact on society.

Public disapproval

In 1937, Goebbels decided that there should be a public exhibition of the most degenerate pieces of art so that people could see them and be repulsed by their corrupt nature. The *Entartete Kunst* (Degenerate Art) exhibition opened in Munich in the summer of 1937 and toured other German cities in the following year. There were over 650 paintings in the exhibition and 'Reife Sonnenblumen' was one of them. The rooms were deliberately chaotic, overfilled with paintings on every surface, many just hung by cord. Among the paintings there were huge slogans painted on to the walls, such as 'Nature as seen by sick minds'.

Nolde's artistic career was over. The official celebration of his seventieth birthday in 1937 was cancelled and, in 1941, the *Reichskammer der Bildenden Kunste* (the ministry in charge of art) took the extreme measure of banning Nolde from painting even in private. As a Nazi Party member, Nolde wrote a letter of appeal to Baron von Schirach, a leading Nazi, but to no avail.

▲ One of Nolde's 'unpainted pictures'. It is called 'Sea in the evening light' and was painted between 1938 and 1945.

Private resistance

But art was Nolde's passion and he knew he would have to paint. Painting with oils was out of the question as the strong distinctive smell would give him away. Nolde began painting with watercolours in secret. He called these his 'unpainted pictures' and hid hundreds of them around his house, proving that the Nazis could not control every aspect of society, even if they so wished.

However, Nolde would not have to wait long to paint again. In 1945, with the collapse of the Nazi regime, Nolde returned to his passion and was soon putting on new exhibitions around Germany. 'Reife Sonnenblumen' could also return to its rightful place. Saved from destruction, the painting is now seen as a classic example of Nolde's work and sits in the Detroit Institute of Art. It is no longer seen as degenerate, but instead as the beautiful painting it has always been.

3

Dem Deutschen Volke

How did the lives of the German people change, 1933–39?

▲ 'The Farming Family from Kalenberg' by Adolf Wissel, 1938

This painting is called 'The Farming Family from Kalenberg'. It was painted by Adolf Wissel in 1938. He tries to show the Nazi ideal of the German family. Every person is of Aryan blood, with blond hair and blue eyes. The father works the land that you can see behind them, while the stay-at-home mother looks after her conventional and obedient children. The mood of the family seems stern and serious. They have no time for frivolous activity. Together they represent the Nazi idea known as 'Blood and Soil': this saw traditional farming families who had faithfully worked the same land for generations as the backbone of the German people, or (in German) *Dem Deutschen Volke*.

Wissel's work was enormously popular among Nazis. His paintings went on display in exhibitions organised by Goebbels' Ministry of Propaganda. Goebbels, Göring and other party leaders bought his paintings. In 1939, this painting of the Kalenberg farming family was bought by Hitler himself. He was a satisfied customer.

The painting is too simple, of course. Very few German families matched this ideal. The lives of the 67 million German people in 1933 were far more complex and far more diverse than those shown in Wissel's painting. By 1939, however, Hitler's government had done its best to change German society into something more like the Aryan ideal. Between 1933 and 1939, the Nazis passed a vast array of laws that affected everyone from the young to the old, no matter what their gender or ethnicity.

In some ways, the changes brought about by Nazi laws and policies made life easier for many Germans. Under the Nazis, unemployment in Germany was virtually eradicated, holidays could be bought at a reduced price and there was a great selection of clubs and activities for the young. But there was a price to pay, as the position of women in society was reduced to child-rearing and home-making, children were brain-washed and the persecution of the Jews and other 'undesirables' began in earnest. The real picture of *Dem Deutschen Volke* was certainly far more complex than the painting suggests.

Reflect

What can Wissel's painting 'The Farming Family from Kalenberg' tell us about life in Nazi Germany, 1933–39?

The Enquiry

Wissel's painting tries to portray the ideal German family according to the Nazis and, as a result, it fails to do justice to the reality of life under Nazi rule. It is just too simple and too limited in what it shows.

In this enquiry, your challenge is to correct some other over-simple summaries of German life between 1933 and 1939. These will not take the form of paintings but will be short sentences or paragraphs. You will have to use what you learn about life under Nazi rule in Germany at this time to amend the statements so that they are closer to the truth.

There are three sections to this enquiry:

1. Nazi policies and their impact on men and women at work and home
2. The lives of young people in Nazi Germany, including education and youth movements
3. Nazi racial policy and the growing persecution of Jews.

At the start of each section, you will be given the 'over-simple summary' of that aspect of life in Germany. At the end of the section, you will be asked to adapt, develop and improve the summary so that it is closer to the truth.

Work and home

This first section considers how life changed under the Nazis for adults at work and at home. See the 'Record' box on the left for guidance on what you need to do.

Workers

On the surface, the Nazis greatly improved life for workers. During the election of 1932, when there were nearly 6 million unemployed, the Nazi manifesto promised to provide jobs. Sure enough, by 1939, unemployment had officially been reduced to 35,000 out of a total of 25 million men. However, behind this statistic lies a more complex picture.

Small craftsmen

Improving business for the *Mittelstand* (or small craftsman) was a key priority for the Nazis. In 1933 the Law to Protect Retail Trade was passed which put increased taxes on large stores to protect these smaller businesses. Despite this, the *Mittelstand* could not compete with larger firms and, between 1936 and 1939, the number of artisans actually fell from 1.6 million to 1.5 million.

Peasants

In line with their belief in 'Blood and Soil', the Nazis made agricultural workers, or peasants, another high priority. In May 1933, the Reich Entailed Farm Law was passed. This aimed to strengthen Germany's small farms by forcing owners to pass the land on to the eldest son rather than divide it up between brothers or sell it to large-scale landowners. Unfortunately, this tied the peasants to the land and stifled innovation. In this period, the rural population fell from 21 per cent of the total population to 18 per cent.

Industrial workers

Industrial workers were a large and growing group, about 46 per cent of the population. The Nazi obsession with re-armament and preparation for war made industrial jobs plentiful and employment rates soared. By 1936, the average wage was 35 marks per week, ten times more than the dole money that the 6 million unemployed had received in 1932. Unfortunately, wages were frozen at 1933 levels and so rising prices meant that they were still not enough to feed a family easily.

On taking power, the Nazis had cut some welfare support provided by the Weimar government but in September 1933 they had to set up their own Winter Relief collection to help the worst off by providing soup stations. Technically, donations were voluntary but constant pressure from the SA meant that on average 3 per cent of a family's income went to the Winter Relief fund. These forced contributions and rising prices meant that being employed did not necessarily mean being comfortable.

Record

Start your first set of notes under the heading 'The impact of Nazi policies on work'. As you read pages 46–47, gather ideas and evidence that will help you to improve the following over-simple summary:

'Between 1933 and 1939, Nazi policies put the German people back to work.'

▲ A Nazi election poster from 1932. The caption says: 'Workers, whether you work with the head or the fist, vote for the soldier who served at the front – Hitler!'

Reflect

1. What does this poster show about Nazi attitudes to work?
2. How is it similar to or different from the painting on page 44?

Deutsche Arbeitsfront (DAF)

After the abolition of the trades unions (see page 19), the Nazis wanted to fill the gap with an organisation to win over the workers. They set up the *Deutsche Arbeitsfront* (DAF), literally meaning German Labour Front. Run by Robert Ley, this was designed 'to create a true social and productive community'. Membership was voluntary but those who did not join struggled to find work. By 1939, there were 29 million members. Workers had to pay to join and through this scheme the Nazis raised a significant income.

The DAF had many different branches and functions. Four of the most important were:

- **Strength through Joy** (*Kraft durch Freude* or KDF) was created to organise workers' leisure time. This included subsidised holidays, cheap theatre tickets, touring orchestras and gym evenings. Each of these activities included ideological content delivered by the Party, for example passengers on the Strength through Joy cruise ships received political lectures. In 1937 alone, 1.7 million went on their package tours and 7 million took short excursions. With a 75 per cent discount on trains and 50 per cent discount on hotels, it is not difficult to see the appeal of this programme even for those who did not wholeheartedly agree with the Nazi ideology.

- **Beauty of Labour** aimed to improve work places. Through this branch, new toilets, changing rooms and showers were built at factories across Germany.

- The **Reich Labour Service** was set up to tackle unemployment by providing cheap labour for big state projects like new motorways. From 1935, all men aged between 18 and 25 had to serve for six months. They were trained along the lines of a military force and took part in Nazi rallies, marching past Hitler with their shovels on their shoulders as if they were soldiers carrying rifles.

- In 1938, the DAF created the **Volkswagen scheme**, which meant that workers could pay 5 marks per week and eventually earn a car. Many paid in to the scheme but no one ever received a car as the Second World War stopped production.

However, the Nazis' pressure for them to respond to all of these initiatives left many workers feeling harassed. By 1939, there was growing disillusionment.

▲ Two cruise liners set off for Madeira carrying German workers on their KDF holidays in 1936. On one, at the front of the photograph, Robert Ley is already delivering a Nazi propaganda message to the passengers.

▶ A Volkswagen Beetle, 1938

Reflect

1. Which aspects of the work of the DAF are represented by the images on this page?
2. What other images might exist that would help a historian to understand the work of the DAF?

Women's lives

Between the end of the First World War and 1933, Germany had shown progressive views towards the lives of women. However, following the Nazi takeover of power in 1933, things changed dramatically.

The Nazis' 'ideal woman'

In 1933, Goebbels perfectly summed up Nazi views on women when he said:

> The mission of the woman is to be beautiful and to bring children into the world … The female bird pretties herself for her mate and hatches the eggs for him.

The artist and SS member Wolfgang Willrich put across a similar message about the role of women in this painting that was copied and published as a poster throughout Germany. The image is filled with signs of fertility.

Through all sorts of propaganda, Nazi views about women were made all too clear. Some of these are listed below.

Nazi views on how women should live

- Women should not smoke, particularly as smoking could lead to a higher chance of miscarriage.
- Women should appear natural and not wear makeup. Cosmetics and hair dyes were seen as a French obsession.
- Women should dress in traditional German clothes and not show sexuality overtly.
- The role of women in the kitchen was crucial. Once a month they should participate in 'One Pot Sunday', making a stew from leftovers to reduce waste. The SA and Block wardens checked that women were fulfilling this duty.
- Women should not be thin but 'physically robust'. Strong women were best for bearing children.
- Women should be members of the National Socialist Women's League. Led by Gertrud Scholtz-Klink, this organisation had 2 million members by 1938 and offered meetings, a bi-weekly magazine and training in domestic duties such as cooking and cleaning.

Despite all these efforts, Nazi ideals did not take root everywhere, as historian Richard J. Evans explains in his 2005 book, *The Third Reich in Power*:

> The cosmetics industry soon found new ways of making profits. Magazines were full of advice to German women on how to achieve a natural look by artificial means. Shampoo companies quickly marketed new products enabling women to achieve a much-desired head of blonde hair. Prominent women in Nazi high society scorned the attack on fashion: Magda Goebbels (Joseph's wife) often appeared in public smoking through a cigarette holder.

Record

Start your second set of notes under the heading 'The impact of Nazi policies on women's lives'. As you read pages 48–49, make notes that will help you to improve this over-simple summary:

'All German women were made to follow the Nazi ideal of motherhood between 1933 and 1939.'

▼ 'Family portrait', painted by Wolfgang Willrich, 1938

Reflect

1. What signs of fertility has Willrich included in the painting above?
2. How useful are the quotation from Goebbels, the painting by Willrich and the interpretation of Richard J. Evans in helping us to understand the home life of women living under Nazi rule?

Policies to encourage motherhood

Hitler's government used its powers to try to create more women who fitted the Nazi ideal. In particular it tried to encourage marriage and motherhood among Aryans at a time when the population of Germany and other European nations was falling. They saw this as essential for producing a new generation of pure Aryan Germans who would serve for the Nazis' 'thousand year' Reich. Motherhood would also keep women at home as the Nazis wanted. Here are three of the methods they tried in order to encourage motherhood between 1933 and 1939:

1 **Loans to encourage women to marry and have children**
   Soon after coming to power in 1933, the government decided to encourage young women to get married and have children rather than take paid employment. It offered loans to Aryan couples who were about to get married. (Non-Aryans were not offered the same loans.) The couple could receive goods of up to 1000 Reichsmarks in value if the woman gave up her job and agreed not to return to work until the loan had been repaid. Goods rather than cash were given to couples as this had the side effect of stimulating German manufacturing.

   As it might take the couple up to eight years to pay off their loan, the woman would be kept out of employment for all that time. To encourage child-bearing, the loan was reduced by a quarter for every child the couple went on to have. This meant that a couple who had four children would not need to repay the loan at all. In 1934, 250,000 loans were issued. In 1937, the requirement for women to give up work was removed in the hope of increasing the rate of marriage and births even further.

2 **Making divorce and re-marriage more easy**
   Divorces were made easier to obtain so women could remarry and have more children.

3 **Reducing opportunities for women in higher education**
   Women's participation in higher education was severely limited. Female enrolment at universities was limited to 10 per cent of all students.

The impact of Nazi policies on women's lives

It is difficult to judge what effects these different policies had.

- **Marriages** did increase from 516,000 in 1932 to 772,000 in 1939.
- **Births** rose in the early 1930s but by 1939 the rate had declined again. The average number of children per couple in 1932 had been 3.6 and by 1939 it had dropped to 3.3.
- The number of **women in employment** increased between 1933 and 1939. This was natural as other Nazi policies helped to create a booming economy in the mid- to late 1930s when jobs were plentiful. In agriculture, 4.6 million women were employed in 1933; by 1939 this had increased to 4.9 million. In industry the figure rose from 2.7 million to 3.3 million.
- The number of **women in higher education** fell. This is the one policy that seemed to have the desired effect, with numbers of women at German universities significantly dropping in this period. The Nazi government came to regret its success, however, in the late 1930s. At that point it needed highly qualified women to take on work caused by the rapid re-armament programme in preparation for war. Women were very reluctant to take places at universities having been discouraged from doing so since 1933.

▼ The Honour Cross of the German Mother was issued to women who had large families. There was a bronze medal for four or five children, silver for six or seven children and gold for eight or more children. Artists such as Willrich (page 48) were ordered to show at least four children in the family scenes they painted.

Record

Use your notes on pages 48–49 to improve the over-simple summary given on page 48.

The lives of young people in Nazi Germany

Last year my family discovered this photograph. It shows my grandfather David. He was British but went on a scouting holiday in Germany in 1938. In the photo, David is performing the *Hitlergrüsse* (Hitler greeting) and is wearing a swastika armband that he had borrowed from a member of the Hitler Youth.

We have no idea why he was doing this. Did doing this make David a Nazi? It is highly unlikely! He was an innocent fourteen-year-old boy who probably did not understand what he was doing. I would imagine that David was just carried away by what he saw and wanted to join in with the community he was visiting.

Photographs like this illustrate the innocence of youth. Young people were easily influenced and the Nazis took advantage of that. As a result, the lives of young Germans were shaped between 1933 and 1939 by school and youth organisations that indoctrinated them with Nazi beliefs and values.

▲ The author's grandfather, David Gummer in Germany in 1938

Record

As you read pages 50–53, make notes that will help you to improve this over-simple summary:

'A whole generation of German youth was controlled by the Nazis between 1933 and 1939.'

Education

The school system was run by Bernhard Rust, the Reich Education Minister, who once said 'The whole function of education is to create Nazis.' Through control of teachers and the curriculum, the Nazis aimed to impose their ideology onto the young.

Controlling teachers

The key to creating a Nazi education system was to control the teachers. After the Nazi takeover of power in 1933, politically unreliable teachers were forced to resign, leaving only those who would follow Nazi orders. In Berlin, 13 per cent of head teachers were fired. Jewish teachers were banned from teaching in non-Jewish schools. A National Socialist (Nazi) Teachers League was established and 97 per cent of all teachers had joined it by 1936. The League ran 'political education' courses for teachers that made them do military-style exercises and learn the latest Nazi ideology.

Teachers who stepped out of line would face the Nazi machinery of terror. Before long, pupils acted as classroom spies and reported to the Gestapo the names of any teacher who still dared to tell anti-Nazi jokes or teach non-Nazi material.

Controlling schools

In addition to controlling teachers in state schools, the Nazis also set up their own schools directly run by the Party.

- Napola or military cadet schools were set up and run by SS and SA officers teaching a military education.
- Adolf Hitler Schools were run by the leaders of the Hitler Youth and were designed to create future leaders of the Party with a focus on physical and military education.

Selection for both of these types of school was based on racial and physical criteria. Unsurprisingly this did not result in the best candidates. By and large, the elite schools were a failure. By 1939 only 6173 pupils were schooled at the sixteen Napola and ten Adolf Hitler Schools.

Controlling the curriculum

From January 1934, it was compulsory for schools to educate children in 'the spirit of National Socialism'. Old textbooks were thrown out and teachers were sent a constant stream of orders about what to teach as they Nazified the curriculum. Below are some examples of how the Nazis expected their values and beliefs to be taught whenever there was an opportunity.

History (*Geschichte*) centred on the struggle between nations and on the superiority of Germany and the Aryan race. Strong leadership was praised for changing the flow of history. The defeat of Germany in the First World War was blamed on the Jews.

Geography (*Erd Kunde*) emphasised pride in Germany and taught about the need for *Lebensraum* (living space) for the German people.

The **physics** (*Flugphÿsik*) curriculum focused on the science of firearms, aerodynamics and radio communications.

Mathematics (*Rechnen*) was often taught in the form of 'social arithmetic'. Pupils were given calculations that filled their minds with Nazi ideas. They would, for example, be asked to work out the cost of keeping a mentally ill patient alive in an asylum.

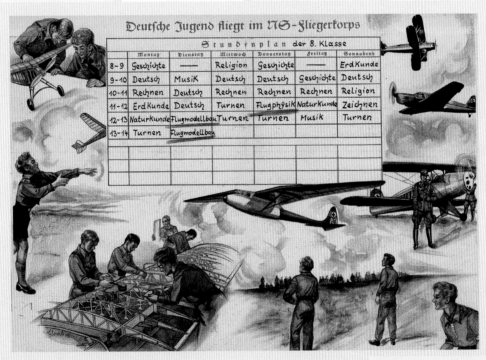

◀ The timetable of a German school. This one is from 1940 and shows the lessons in a boys' military cadet school linked to the airforce.

German (*Deutsch*) lessons explained how the language had developed from a specific Aryan racial background.

Religious education (*Religion*) was greatly reduced. In 1937, it became an optional subject.

PE (*Turnen*) lessons took up at least 15 per cent of all lesson time as the Nazis believed it was crucial to keep people fit, healthy and ready for a war.

Biology (part of *Naturkunde*) was focused on *Rassenkunde*, the study of race. Girls were taught how to identify ideal Aryan husbands. Some lessons encouraged pupils to measure the features of the non-Aryan children in the class.

Reflect

Academic standards dropped in the 1930s. Why do you think this was?

Youth organisations

As well as trying to control school life, the Nazis also tried to control young people's leisure time. In Germany there had always been a strong history of youth organisations or clubs providing leisure, sport and entertainment in the evenings and at weekends.

In the late 1920s, the Nazis set up their own youth organisation, the Hitler Youth. It was run by Baldur von Schirach and had four parts. There were different sections for girls and boys, with juniors aged between ten and fourteen and seniors aged fourteen to eighteen.

At first, membership of Hitler Youth was voluntary. However, after 1936 it was made compulsory for young people to join and after 1939 it was compulsory for members to attend meetings.

In addition to this, the Nazis began shutting down other youth groups and after 1936 the Hitler Youth was the only organisation through which young people could access sports facilities and activities.

Meetings for both boys and girls focused on indoctrination and physical activities. Commonly they sang political songs, read Nazi books and paraded through towns. Boys' activities were often more focused on preparation for the military, with activities such as Morse code tests, map reading and even firing rifles loaded with live ammunition. Girls' groups concentrated on domestic duties and even military nursing. For both boys and girls there was the possibility of going on holiday camps. This was particularly attractive to the working classes.

◀ A set of toy Hitler Youth models for children to play with at home, made in Germany, c.1935. Similar models were made of soldiers, SA stormtroopers and Hitler himself. His right arm could be raised in a Hitler salute.

One young boy, Henry Metelmann, joined the Hitler Youth in 1933. In 1992, in his autobiography, this is how he recalled his time:

From *A Hitler Youth: Growing Up in Germany in the 1930s*

Even though father hated everything connected with the Nazis, I liked it in the Hitler Youth. I thought the uniform was smashing, the dark brown, the black, the swastika and all the shiny leather. Where before we seldom had a decent football to play with, the Hitler Youth provided us with decent sports equipment, and previously out-of-bounds gymnasiums, swimming pools and even stadiums were now open to us.

Never in my life had I been on a real holiday – father was much too poor for such an extravagance. Now under Hitler, for very little money I could go on lovely camps in the mountains, by the rivers or near the sea.

… The songs we sung were beautifully melodic, all about our great race, our Lebensraum in the East, and the glory of fighting and dying for our Fatherland. I liked the comradeship, the marching, the sport and the war games. We were brought up to love our Führer, who was to me like a second God, and when we were told about his great love for us, the German nation, I was often close to tears. I was convinced that because of the German blood in my veins that I was a superior being.

▼ Membership of the Hitler Youth, 1932–39

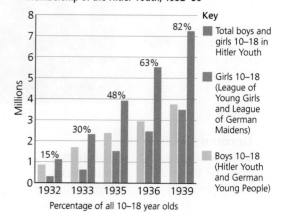

Percentage of all 10–18 year olds

Key
- Total boys and girls 10–18 in Hitler Youth
- Girls 10–18 (League of Young Girls and League of German Maidens)
- Boys 10–18 (Hitler Youth and German Young People)

Reflect

Henry Metelmann says that Hitler was 'like a second God'. Why do you think he had such extreme feelings?

▲ Members of the League of German Girls (the older age group) performing a traditional German dance, c.1938

Limited impact

Not every child was so convinced by Nazi propaganda in schools and in the Hitler Youth. Many were bored or resentful at the meetings, especially those who usually avoided physical activity. Others enjoyed parts of the programme but resisted the political messages. Some just hated being forced to attend.

In 2011, an American citizen who had grown up in Germany in the 1930s published a book that was based on interviews with others who had shared that experience. In an interview about his book he summarised how the impact of Nazi propaganda was limited:

▲ Members of the senior boys Hitler Youth hiking in southern Germany, c.1935

From an interview with Frederic C. Tubach,
German voices: Memories of life during Hitler's
Third Reich, 2011

Family, school, and church: these three forces worked on us too. It varied with individual experience. But in school there was, for the most part, not much difference from the Weimar Republic and earlier.

… Some Nazi teachers wanted us to read about Germanic myths. But we weren't examined on their preferences. Most of us read what students had always read. We had to belong [to Hitler Youth] and there were meetings twice a week, but what the leaders said was emotional and inconsistent. Family was more important for most of us. If the family was anti-Nazi, the odds were that the child would be too … People from a religious family usually had a kind of protective coating: 'Christ is more important than Hitler'. They might only think it or say it under their breath, but many felt it.

Reflect

What reasons can you find on this page for young people sometimes resisting the effects of Nazi propaganda?

Record

Use your notes on pages 50–53 to improve the over-simple summary given on page 50.

▶ A statue of a perfect Aryan, by Arno Breker, 1938

 # Nazi racial policy: the growing persecution of Jews

The Nazis were obsessed by race. They believed there were distinct races of people and that some were stronger or better than others. This statue by Arno Breker used to stand by the door of the Reich Chancellery. It celebrated the Nazis' pride in the perfect physical form of the Aryan peoples of northern Europe.

At the other extreme, in Nazi minds, were the Jews whose supposed inferiority led to their persecution and ultimately to the Holocaust. In this part of the enquiry, you will learn why the Nazis believed in this racial theory and discover how the persecution of the Jews evolved between 1933 and 1939.

Record

As you read pages 54–58, make notes that will help you to improve this over-simple summary:

'On gaining power in 1933, Hitler unleashed a sudden, new and violent persecution of Germany's Jewish population.'

Übermenschen

Hitler and other Nazis had made their feelings about race very clear for many years before gaining power. Hitler's book, *Mein Kampf*, was filled with anti-Semitism. Taking inspiration from nineteenth-century German philosophers and scientists, Nazis believed the strongest and best of the races were the Aryans, the people of northern and western Europe. They saw Aryans as *Übermenschen*, meaning super humans or the master race. Strong, athletic Aryans were represented in Nazi art and propaganda. Nazis believed that Germany would only regain its strength if it were exclusively filled with, and run by, Aryans.

Leading scientists like Hans F.K. Günther who influenced Nazi policy, taught that there were distinct types of Aryan who shared the same features – for example, size of head or nose, colour of eyes or hair. Posters like this one were used to show the typical features of each group. The most superior type of Aryan was the Nordic group with blond hair and blue eyes. Of course, Hitler did not have blond hair and blue eyes. He could not claim to be one of the Nordic type but he was still an Aryan.

Reflect

Look at the poster. Which type of Aryan do you think Hitler would have claimed to be?

Bilder deutscher Rassen 1

Formen: Sehr großwüchsig, schlank, langköpfig, schmalgesichtig, Nase schmal, Haar wellig.

Nordische Rasse

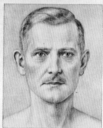

Farben: Sehr hell, Haar goldblond, Augen blau bis grau, Haut rosig-weiß.

Formen: Sehr großwüchsig, wuchtig, langköpfig, breitgesichtig, Nase ziemlich schmal, Haar wellig oder lockig.

Fälische Rasse

Farben: Hell, Haar blond, Augen blau bis grau, Haut rosig-weiß.

Formen: Kleinwüchsig, schlank, langköpfig, mittelbreitgesichtig, Nase ziemlich schmal, Haar wellig oder lockig.

Westische Rasse

Farben: Sehr dunkel, Haar schwarz, Augen schwarz, Haut hellbraun.

▲ This poster (1935) shows just three of the types within the Aryan race – the Nordic, the Phalian and the Western

Untermenschen

The Nazis believed that non-Aryans were inferior and called them *Untermenschen* or sub-humans. The term was used to describe a wide range of people including Gypsies, black people and Slavs (people from eastern Europe such as Poland and Russia). Slavs were also called *Düngervolk*, or dung-people. But the Nazis' most vicious hatred was reserved for the group that they saw as the lowest of the low: the Jews.

To be defined as Jewish, a person did not have to hold Jewish beliefs. Everything depended on ancestry. According to the Nuremberg Laws of 1935, anyone with three or four grandparents who were Jewish was also Jewish. Those with one or two grandparents who were Jewish were called *Mischling* or half-Jews.

The Nazis believed that races had distinct facial features and that Jews and Gypsies, in particular, could be identified by their large noses. To aid their research into racial types, they measured Jewish people's noses precisely.

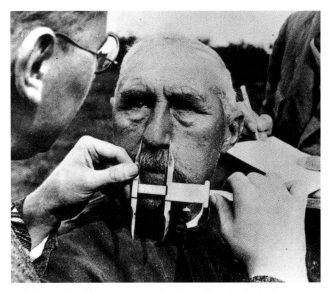

▲ A German has his nose measured to determine whether he is a Jew, 1940

Dangerous myths

After their first, early actions against the Jews in the spring of 1933 (see pages 17–18), the Nazis toned down the official persecution in the next few months, waiting to judge the reaction from the wider population and the international community. It did, however, carry on spreading a wide range of myths and misinformation about Jewish life, helping to stir up German fear and hatred. Some of these myths are shown below along with a more balanced view based on historical research.

Nazi myth: There was a long, continuous history of widespread anti-Semitism in Germany.

Reality: Although the roots of anti-Semitism went back to the Middle Ages, by 1933 Jews were fully integrated into German society. Marriages with non-Jews, for example, were quite common.

Nazi myth: Jews were racially inferior.

Reality: There is no scientific evidence to support this. There is a single 'race' of humans.

Nazi myth: Jews owned the big businesses in Germany and profited from the economic problems of the 1920s and early 1930s.

Reality: Some Jews did own big business, but they did not own all of them. Jews belonged to all classes of society from the workers to the upper class.

The Jews of Germany – Nazi myths and historical reality

Nazi myth: Germany was dominated by Jews who controlled the country.

Reality: In 1933, there were only 505,000 Jews out of a population of 67 million. Their influence was very limited. In the previous Weimar government only a few key ministers were Jewish.

Nazi myth: Jews were cowards and pacifists. Their refusal to fight for Germany helped to cause its defeat in 1918.

Reality: Jews fought in the German army in the same way as other citizens. Some even received the Iron Cross for bravery.

Nazi myth: Jews were Communists. They had led the revolution in Russia in 1917 and would lead a revolution in Germany.

Reality: Although some leading Communists were Jews, German Jews belonged to the full spectrum of political parties.

Social persecution, humiliation and violence

The growing mood of fear and suspicion of Jews meant they faced all sorts of social persecution at the hands of some of their German neighbours. You saw how this began with the boycott of Jewish businesses in April 1933 (see page 17). Boycotts continued from that time onwards and persecution became more intense as the years passed, showing itself in many different ways.

Social exclusion was common by 1935. Signs like this one saying 'Jews not wanted here' appeared in public places such as parks, shops and restaurants, increasingly isolating the Jewish population from the rest of the German people.

◀ 'Jews not wanted here' sign from Germany, c.1935

Although **physical persecution** was not as common in this period as it was later in the war years, Jews still lived in fear of mistreatment. In March 1933, in the city of Munich, a Jew had his windows smashed by the SA. His lawyer, Michael Siegel, complained to the police about the attack. They did not listen. Instead they beat Siegel and forced him to walk through the Munich streets barefoot with a sign saying 'I will never again complain to the police'. Many Jews in other cities faced similar experiences, especially during the summer of 1935.

▶ Jewish lawyer Michael Siegel being forced to march through the streets of Munich in 1933

Publications throughout the period portrayed Jews as money grabbers and communists intent on bringing about the destruction of Germany. Nazi newspapers like *Der Stürmer* (see page 32) regularly printed horrific anti-Semitic cartoons showing Jews as paedophiles and rapists.

Even some children's books were deeply anti-Semitic. This book is called the *Der Giftpilz* (*The Toadstool*). It was published in 1938 by Julius Streicher, the same man who edited *Der Stürmer*. It described Jews as poisonous mushrooms and told the children that 'Just as a single poisonous mushroom can kill a whole family, so a solitary Jew can destroy a whole village, a whole city, even an entire nation'.

◀ The front cover of an anti-Semitic children's story book, 1938

Most of this active anti-Semitism came from Nazi grassroots supporters, but as one Social Democrat supporter observed in 1935:

The persecution of the Jews is not meeting with any active support from the population. On the other hand, it is not completely failing to make an impression. Unnoticed, racial propaganda is leaving its traces. People are losing their impartiality towards the Jews.

Kristallnacht

The most extreme outbreak of violence against German Jews took place on 9 and 10 November 1938. The attacks on Jewish homes and businesses were so brutal that the shattered glass in the streets all over Germany gave it the name *Kristallnacht* or The Night of Broken Glass. Nothing was the same in Germany after this.

The trigger for the attacks came on 7 November when a seventeen-year-old Polish Jew, Herschel Grynszpan, assassinated a German embassy official, Ernst Vom Rath, in Paris. Grynszpan was acting in protest against the German policy of forcing Polish Jews to emigrate from Germany.

When the news of the murder reached Germany, there was widespread anger at the Jewish population. On 9 November, the Nazi leaders met in Munich to decide how to respond. Goebbels announced that 'the Führer has decided that … demonstrations should not be prepared or organised by the Party, but insofar as they erupt spontaneously, they are not to be hampered'. In other words the Nazis were not directly organising attacks on the Jews but if such attacks happened they should not be stopped. This message was conveyed to local Nazi parties and many SA and Hitler Youth groups took this as an official invitation to unleash violence. These were government-organised attacks in all but name.

From the evening of 9 November and into the early hours of the next day, 267 synagogues were destroyed and 7500 Jewish-owned commercial establishments had their windows smashed and contents looted. At least 91 Jews were murdered and police records show a high number of associated rapes and suicides. At the same time, in a move that was clearly planned, the SS and Gestapo arrested up to 30,000 Jewish men and sent most of them to concentration camps. This was the first time Jews had been imprisoned en masse. Many died in the following weeks due to the horrific conditions in which they were kept.

Whether through fear or silent agreement, the German public did not speak out against these attacks on Jews and, to a large extent, nor did the wider world.

Reflect

Why do you think most historians see *Kristallnacht* as the beginning of the Holocaust?

▲ Smashed windows of a looted Jewish-owned shop in Berlin, 10 November 1938

Anti-Semitic legislation, 1933–39

The first duty of a government is to protect the people it serves. The Nazi government of Germany, however, not only failed to protect the Jews, it actively persecuted them. The Nazi government took no action against those who committed acts such as those you have just read about on pages 56–57. Instead, it used the legislative power of the state against the Jews. Between 1933 and 1939, the Nazis passed hundreds of anti-Semitic laws. Many are listed below. The 'Reflect' activities help you to understand how these laws gradually destroyed Jewish rights.

March 1933	Jewish lawyers are banned from conducting legal affairs in Berlin. Jewish judges are suspended from office.
April 1933	Aryan and non-Aryan children are forbidden from playing together. Jews are excluded from sport and gymnastics clubs.
July 1933	Jews are excluded from the German Chess Federation.
August 1933	Jews are excluded from choirs.
September 1933	'Race studies' become part of the school examination syllabus.
March 1935	Jewish musicians are not allowed to practise their profession. Jewish writers are not allowed to engage in any form of literary activity.
July 1935	Young Jews are not allowed to go hiking in groups of more than twenty.
September 1935 (the Nuremberg Laws)	Marriages and extra marital intercourse between nationals of German stock and Jews are punishable by imprisonment. Jews are no longer 'citizens'; they are just 'subjects' with no rights.
January 1936	Jews must hand over all electrical equipment, bicycles, typewriters and records.
April 1936	Jewish veterinary surgeons are banned from practising. Only Aryans can work as journalists.
October 1936	Jews who convert to Christianity are still to be treated as Jews.
April 1937	Jews are forbidden to obtain a doctorate.
June 1937	Post Office officials married to a Jewess are forced into retirement.
January 1938	Jews are banned from belonging to the German Red Cross.
March 1938	Jews are banned from being allotment holders.

Reflect

Why do you think these early laws restricted Jewish involvement in the legal professions?

Reflect

Some of the earlier reforms seem quite trivial. Does this mean they did not matter?

Reflect

Why are the Nuremberg Laws of 1935 such a turning point?

April 1938	Jews must show how much they own to ensure that their wealth is being used in the interest of the German economy.
July 1938	Jewish doctors are not allowed to practise on non-Jewish patients. Jewish street names are changed.
August 1938	Male Jews must add 'Israel' and female Jews 'Sara' to their first names.
October 1938	Jewish passports have to be stamped with a 'J' and passports belonging to Jews whose emigration is undesirable are to be confiscated.
November 1938 (at the time of *Kristallnacht*, see page 57)	All Jewish children are expelled from non-Jewish state schools. Jews are no longer allowed to buy newspapers and magazines. Jews are banned from running businesses as craftsmen. Jews are banned from running retail or wholesale businesses. Jews are banned from cinemas, theatres, operas and concerts.
December 1938	Jewish driving licences must be handed over. Jews are not allowed to use swimming pools. Jewish publishing houses and bookshops are closed down. Jews are not allowed to attend university. Jewish women are refused recognition as midwives.
January 1939	Jewish emigrants are not allowed to take valuables with them. Jews can no longer work as dentists, chemists, nurses or in other medical posts.
February 1939	Jews have to hand over jewellery, gold, silver and pearls.
March 1939	Jews have to remove the ruins of synagogues destroyed by rioters. Reconstruction is not permitted.
April 1939	Jews can be evicted from their homes without a reason being given.
September 1939	Jews are no longer allowed to leave their homes after 8 p.m. (or 9 p.m. in the summer).

Reflect

Why do you think the Nazis wanted to be able to identify Jews quickly and easily?

Reflect

Jewish property was first taken by the state in 1939. Why were the Nazis confident that they could get away with this by 1939?

Reflect

Look back through the timeline and find all the jobs that Jews could no longer do. What does this suggest about how they were living by 1939?

No escape

Under the growing persecution, 282,000 Jews chose to emigrate from Germany between 1933 and 1939. They had to pay a heavy emigration tax and, by 1939, they had to leave almost all their possessions behind. Most moved to neighbouring countries only to find the Nazis followed them as the German armies swept through Europe during the Second World War. By that point, they had nowhere else to run.

Record

Use your notes on pages 54–59 to improve the over-simple summary given on page 54.

Review

Why is it important to challenge over-simple summaries about Hitler's Germany?

The life of Rukeli Trollmann

A closer look at one person's life can often give us a deeper understanding of events in the past. Studying Nazi Germany is no different.

Born in 1907 in Hanover, Johann Trollmann, a champion boxer, should have been hailed as a hero. Instead he was persecuted by the Nazi regime before being murdered in 1944. His story reveals the nightmare of living in Nazi Germany for anyone who was considered different. In Johann's case, he was a Sinti. This was a group of the Romani people and so Johann was considered *untermensch* in the eyes of the Nazis.

The dancing tree

During the 1920s, Johann or Rukeli, which was his boxing nickname (*rukeli* means 'like a tree' in Romani), became a famous fighter, developing a dancing style that at the time was seen as un-German but today is common among boxers. In 1933, Jews were banned from boxing, which led to the light heavyweight title coming up for grabs.

The champion

On 9 June, Rukeli seized his chance when he faced the Aryan champion Adolf Witt for the title. He landed blow after blow against his opponent and was clearly winning the fight. However, the pro-Nazi referee stopped the bout and called a draw. The Nazis could not let a Sinti win. The supporting crowd was furious and the referee was forced to give Rukeli the title.

Three weeks later, however, Rukeli, the 'Gypsy in the ring' as the Nazi press called him, was told that the title had been taken from him and he would have to fight again to prove his worth.

On 21 July, Rukeli would fight the Nazi favourite, Gustav Elder. Rukeli knew he would not be allowed to win so decided to make a stand. Stepping in to the ring with his hair dyed blonde and his face whitened with flour, Rukeli was directly mocking the Nazi ideology. Knowing he had no chance of victory, he allowed his opponent to land punches without defence. He lasted five rounds before collapsing. Rukeli's career was over. Unfortunately, the sad story of Johann Trollmann was not.

Obscurity

There is little evidence of what happened to Johann in the years 1933–38 as it appears he went into hiding to avoid persecution. In the late 1930s, Sinti increasingly began to suffer persecution similar to the Jews. Some Sinti, including Johann, were given a straight choice: either go to a concentration camp or be sterilised (an operation that stops you from having children). Records show Johann took the latter option and, in 1938, divorced his non-Sinti wife to protect her and their daughter.

Duty

In 1939, Germany invaded Poland and the Second World War began. In what could be considered a surprising act, Johann joined the *Wehrmacht* (Germany army) and spent the next three years fighting for the country that had treated him so badly. Johann was not the only Sinti to join up, showing that the Nazi obsession with race could be turned aside when strong fighters were offering their services (although this was never the case for Jews).

Rejection

1942 was a turning point in the Nazi treatment of Jews and Gypsies, who were no longer tolerated and would now be exterminated.

Johann was discharged from the army and sent to Neuengamme concentration camp in Germany, where all the prisoners were forced to complete back-breaking manual labour tasks. Johann's task was harder though. Recognised by one of the camp guards who was a boxing fan, he was forced to train troops at night after the hard day's work. Doing double the work of any other inmate, Johann was soon near breaking point.

Twice dead

Seeing him deteriorate, the prisoners' committee pulled off a remarkable feat by faking his death and getting him sent to another camp under a false identity. Unfortunately, it was not long before he was recognised again. A fight was arranged between Johann and Emil Cornelius, a hated Kapo who helped run the camp for the SS guards. Cornelius was no match for the ex-boxer and walked away with his pride severely damaged after a severe beating. It was not long before he took his revenge, forcing Johann to work so hard that he was physically exhausted. Waiting until Johann was at his lowest, Cornelius attacked and murdered him with a shovel.

Restoration

There is no happy ending to a story this sad. But there is some justice. In 2003, the German boxing authority posthumously returned the 1933 title to Rukeli. He was once again the victor.

◀ Johann 'Rukeli' Trollmann, c.1933

4

Germany in war

What was the impact of the Second World War on the German people?

On Friday 1 September 1939, people all over Germany woke up and turned on the radio to listen to music. Instead, they heard the voice of Adolf Hitler. The *Führer* informed the German people that at four o'clock in the morning German troops had invaded Poland. One boy later recalled, 'With that our worst fears are realised: it is war'.

At around ten o'clock that morning, Hitler was driven the short distance from the Reich Chancellery to the Kroll Opera House where the German Parliament had met since the Reichstag Fire in 1933. Inside, the Reichstag deputies were seated in the stalls and tiers of the opera house. As you can see in the photograph below, the wings of an enormous Nazi eagle are stretched across what had been the stage. Rays of sun radiated from the swastika in the eagle's claws.

From his high-backed seat in front of the eagle, Göring, the Reichstag President, gave a brief introduction, and Hitler then addressed the Reichstag deputies. He revealed what most people already knew: that Germany was at war with Poland. Hitler gave a justification for the war and went on to explain that huge sacrifices would now be required from the German people. At the end, there was the usual chorus of *Sieg Heils* and Hitler left the Kroll Opera House. As he returned to the Reich Chancellery, Hitler was met by a small and subdued crowd. There was none of the usual cheering. Some people silently raised their right arms in a Nazi salute. One eye witness later recalled hearing the sound of women weeping.

▼ Hitler announcing the invasion of Poland at the Reichstag, 1 September 1939

German people reacted to the news of the outbreak of war with a mixture of emotions. Most Germans, particularly those who remembered the horrors of the 1914–18 conflict, had no desire for another war. Some people showed little concern, assuming that German forces would quickly defeat the Poles. Others were more fearful. One seventeen-year-old schoolgirl recalled the mood on a Berlin train the morning war was announced: 'I remember that we all sat there with these frightfully serious faces. We were depressed. We had the feeling that something terrible was coming'.

And something terrible did come. In the autumn of 1939, the invasion of Poland escalated into a war across Europe. By the end of 1941, it had spread to other parts of the world. During six years of war, from the invasion of Poland in 1939 to the final defeat and surrender of Germany in May 1945, the lives of people around the world would be transformed. The war would lead to unimaginable suffering and to the deaths of millions, including hundreds of thousands of German civilians killed in Allied bombing raids.

Today, Germany remembers the war and its impact on the German people at Neue Wache, the national memorial in Berlin. Inside, the entire space is empty except for a single large bronze statue in the centre. Käthe Kollwitz's 'Mother with her Dead Son' depicts a German mother weeping over the body of her child. Above the statue, an open circle in the roof allows light, rain and snow to fall on the figures below. Underneath are the words, *Den Opfern von Krieg und Gewaltherrschaft* (for the victims of war and tyranny). The statue is a powerful symbol of the loss and suffering endured by the German people during the Second World War.

▲ Käthe Kollwitz's 'Mother with her Dead Son' at the Neue Wache, Berlin

The Enquiry

Your challenge in this enquiry is to plan a new one-hour TV documentary about the impact of the Second World War on the German people. The programme will be divided into three parts:

1. The changing lives of the German people, 1939–42
2. Opposition to the Nazis during the war years
3. The move to 'total war' in the period 1943–45

For each part of the programme, you will need to:

● decide on the content (events, developments and people) which you think should be included

● give the programme researchers some ideas about the possible sources (film clips, photographs, documents, buildings) which you would like them to search for.

For each part of the programme, you should complete a planning sheet like the one below:

Content	Sources

Changing lives, 1939–42

The outbreak of war had an immediate impact on the lives of German people. Fearing bombing raids from Britain, many Berliners headed for the shops to stock up on food and other necessities. Sandbags were distributed and were stacked against ground-floor windows to protect against bomb blasts. In the evening, air raid sirens sounded in Berlin for the first time. No bombs fell, but many inhabitants of the city were gripped with fear. Blackout regulations were issued on the first morning of the conflict. To protect German towns and cities from air attack, no light was to be visible from a height of 500 metres. Kerbstones were painted white and luminous arrows appeared on walls, pointing people to the nearest air raid shelter. Some parents immediately sent their children to live with friends and relatives in the country. Those children who remained in cities were issued with civilian gas masks.

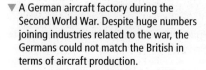

▲ Children receiving a lesson on the use of their civilian gas masks, Berlin, 1939

The move to a war economy

When the Nazis invaded Poland on 1 September 1939, they had prepared for a limited war. After all, in the previous year they had been allowed to invade Czechoslovakia without any interference. Things were different in 1939, however. Within three days, both the British and French had declared war on Germany in support of Poland. The war quickly escalated and German forces made rapid advances into western Europe. In April 1940, German troops marched into Denmark and Norway. The following month, the British withdrew their army from Dunkirk. By June 1940, Belgium and France had both fallen and German aircraft began to target the airfields of Britain.

▼ A German aircraft factory during the Second World War. Despite huge numbers joining industries related to the war, the Germans could not match the British in terms of aircraft production.

To fight on this scale required a huge increase in the supply of weapons and ammunition. In December 1939, Hitler announced that Germany would become a war economy. All industries would focus on supporting the war effort and there would be ambitious targets for every aspect of war production. Military expenditure rose dramatically. In 1939, 23 per cent of the goods produced in German factories were related to the military; by 1941 this had risen to 47 per cent. Huge numbers of German people moved into jobs linked to the war economy. By 1941, 55 per cent of the German workforce was employed in war-related work.

Despite these figures, the war economy in the early years struggled to turn the increased investment into sufficient production. Five different groups tried to control the economy: the SS, the *Wehrmacht*, the *Luftwaffe*, the Navy and local Nazi leaders. Inefficiency and a lack of central control meant that Hitler's advanced war economy had not materialised by the end of 1941.

Albert Speer

Things changed in February 1942 with the appointment of Albert Speer as Minister of Armaments and War Production. Speer was Hitler's personal architect and now took charge of improving the German war economy. As a trusted ally of Hitler, Speer had the power to do what he wanted. The *Führer* famously told him, 'Speer, I'll sign anything that comes from you'.

Speer's plan was to give factories independence, what he called 'industrial self-responsibility', but at the same time ensure central control. In April 1942, he created the Central Planning Board which established greater freedoms for industry but which was ultimately under his direction. Speer encouraged industrialists to join his ministerial team and, where possible, excluded the military personnel who had caused inefficiency in the early years. In addition to giving factories more autonomy, his main policies were to:

- focus factories on producing a single product
- employ more women in factories
- use concentration camp prisoners as workers
- exclude skilled workers from compulsory military service.

	1940	1941	1942	1943	1944
Tanks	1,600	3,800	6,300	12,100	19,000
Aircraft	10,200	11,000	14,200	25,200	39,600

▲ Number of German tanks and aircraft produced, 1940–44

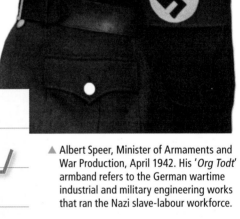

▲ Albert Speer, Minister of Armaments and War Production, April 1942. His '*Org Todt*' armband refers to the German wartime industrial and military engineering works that ran the Nazi slave-labour workforce.

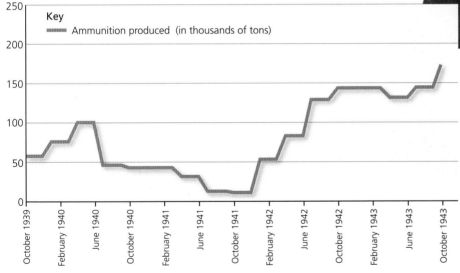

▲ Ammunition production, October 1939 to October 1943

Reflect

1. What can the table of statistics and the graph tell us about the impact of Speer's plan?
2. What questions do they make you want to ask?

The impact of the war on German civilians, 1939–42

The first winter of the war was the coldest in living memory. In January 1940, daytime temperatures across northern Germany rarely rose above –5 °C. Freezing temperatures and heavy snowfall made travel almost impossible. Railway points froze and the waterways were blocked by ice. In these conditions, the most immediate difficulty people faced was a lack of coal. All factories not engaged in war production were told that they would receive no coal. Many businesses, schools, beer halls and cafés were forced to close. The inhabitants of German towns and cities struggled to heat their homes. People foraged for firewood in the parks and forests. Some people had no heating at all and simply wore their outdoor winter clothes indoors.

▲ This poster from 1942 says 'Hamster, shame on you!' Hamsters hoard items of food and this poster was designed to encourage people not to hoard.

Shortages

In the spring of 1940, Germany began to thaw, but the war economy led to serious shortages of food and other products throughout the war years. The Nazis immediately realised that they could not rely on imports and that their own agricultural production would be greatly reduced with so many men in the armed forces. Rationing was therefore introduced from the outset.

The supply of most foods, clothing, shoes and coal was strictly controlled. The German system of rationing was extremely complicated and often caused confusion. People were allocated points according to their age and occupation, and were given colour-coded ration cards for different products. These were re-issued every month so that the authorities could revise the allocation according to supply. The ration cards of German Jews were marked with a red 'J'. Jews were given a much lower allocation and could only shop at certain times, usually half an hour before stores closed, when most goods had already been sold.

The German system of rationing ensured that most people were adequately fed during the war, but German civilians spent much time queuing and the quality of products was much reduced. Complaining could be dangerous. When a Berlin woman described skimmed milk as 'slop' she was reported to the authorities. Her punishment was to report to the police station every day for three months and repeat aloud in front of officials and police officers: 'There is no skimmed milk. There is only de-creamed fresh milk.'

Women

The Nazi leadership was divided over the role of women in the war effort. Speer wanted them to work in the factories to boost production, but Hitler and others still believed they should remain at home to continue their role as wives and mothers. This disagreement meant women were never conscripted into factories as they were in Britain. Despite this, the perception of women did shift during this period, particularly for young women, and they began to be seen as more than wives and mothers. The restrictions on women in education from the early Nazi period were lifted during the war. From 1939, women aged under 25 had to complete six months Labour Service before being allowed to enter full employment. Most women worked their six months in agricultural jobs.

With the restrictions on marriage loans (see page 49) lifted for people in work, more women entered the workforce. In 1939, 760,000 women worked in war industries and this had risen to 1.5 million by 1941. However, the total number of German women aged 15 to 65 was nearly 30 million. With men away at war it seemed that most women preferred to stay at home.

Bombing and evacuation

As the German armies marched across northern France in the spring of 1940, the RAF began a bombing campaign against industrial areas in the north and west of Germany. On 28 August, British planes made a first devastating attack on Berlin. During the autumn of 1940, people in many cities were faced with air raids three or four nights each week. The German government introduced a massive programme to build air raid shelters and to improve air defences in the cities. Night after night, people sought protection in the air raid shelters, but they were not always safe. For example, at the end of October, fifteen Berliners were killed when their air raid shelter collapsed.

In September 1940, the Nazis became increasingly concerned about the safety of German children in the cities. They therefore introduced a programme of evacuation known as *Kinderlandverschickung* – KLV. This system of voluntary evacuation to the countryside was first applied to the cities of Hamburg and Berlin, which were considered to be most at risk from attack. All children below the age of fourteen were eligible for a six-month stay in a rural area. Those below the age of ten were placed in families and could be accompanied by their mothers. Older children were placed in 'camps', which were run by the Hitler Youth.

Conditions in the camps varied enormously. The buildings could be hotels, country houses, monasteries or youth hostels. The camps were often run to a rigid daily timetable and discipline could be very strict.

▲ Women in a German arms factory, 1942

By removing children from their parents for long periods of time, the KLV programme allowed the Nazis to extend their indoctrination of German children during the war years. For this reason, many parents were reluctant to let their children go. Of the 260,000 eligible children in Berlin, only 40,000 participated.

▼ Ten- and eleven-year-old boys at a home of the Hitler Youth, during the preparatory service for their admission to the German Youth, April 1941

Record

Write a planning sheet for the first part of your documentary programme 'The changing lives of the German people, 1939–42' like the one below. A first suggestion has been included to get you started.

The changing lives of the German people, 1939–42	
Content	Sources
Immediate impact: • fear of aerial bombing (blackout, sandbags, children sent to country) • rationing	Photographs of people on streets of German cities, 1939 (e.g. queuing for food, painting kerbstones) Interview with someone who remembers the range of people's reactions to Hitler's announcement of war

Wartime opposition

In Enquiry 2 you learned about the opposition to the Nazis in the period 1933–39. During the war, some German people continued to oppose the Nazi regime. As the terror of the Nazi state intensified, and its policy towards the Jews turned to genocide, various individuals and groups risked their lives in opposition. Some attempted to assassinate Hitler. Others spoke out publicly against the Nazis or wrote critical leaflets and postcards. Unknown numbers of Germans showed their opposition to the regime in minor acts of defiance.

Assassination attempts

The most dramatic opposition to the Nazi regime during the war years were the plots to murder Hitler and other leading Nazis. These often came from elements within the German army. In 1943, when the war was going badly for the Nazis, there were four attempts to assassinate Hitler led by army officers. All these failed, but the following year an assassination attempt almost succeeded ...

The July 1944 bomb plot

The plot was led by Colonel Claus Graf von Stauffenberg, a member of the German nobility and an army officer who agreed with many of the Nazi's nationalistic policies. However, as the war progressed, Stauffenberg became disillusioned with the Nazi leadership and particularly disagreed with the policy towards Jews. Following his injuries fighting the Allies in Tunisia in 1942 (he lost his left eye, his right hand and two fingers on his left hand), Stauffenberg became convinced that Germany was being led into disaster and that the only way to stop this was by removing Hitler.

Reflect

As you find out about the different forms of opposition, don't forget to think about what to include in the second part of your documentary programme.

▲ Claus Graf von Stauffenberg, aristocrat and military officer

During his recovery in Germany, von Stauffenberg came into contact with other people who shared his views. He joined a resistance group led by Ludwig Beck and Henning von Tresckow, and took charge of planning and leading an assassination attempt. The plan was to kill Hitler and initiate Operation Valkyrie, an emergency order which would allow the plotters to use the reserve army to remove the SS and the Gestapo.

By the summer of 1944, time was running out as the Gestapo was closing in on the group. On 1 July, Stauffenberg was appointed Chief of Staff to the Reserve Army. This put him in a position where he had direct contact with the *Führer* on a regular basis. The plan was to bring a case full of explosives to a meeting with Hitler, set it to detonate and escape before it exploded.

Two attempts in early July were aborted, but on 20 July Stauffenberg made another attempt. The meeting took place at Hitler's East Prussian headquarters at Rastenburg. At 12.30 p.m., shortly after the meeting began, Stauffenberg excused himself. In the washroom he fixed a detonator into explosive contained in a case. Returning to the meeting, he slid the case under the table near to Hitler. Stauffenberg then received a planned telephone call and made his exit.

At 12.40 p.m. the bomb detonated. Hearing the explosion, Stauffenberg believed he had been successful and flew back to Berlin to take charge of the wider coup against the Nazis. But the explosion had not killed its target. A heavy table leg had deflected the blast from Hitler. The power of the bomb was less than expected, partly because the meeting had been moved from a concrete bunker to a more open space due to the summer heat.

Back in Berlin, Stauffenberg heard on the radio that Hitler was alive. That evening, he and his fellow-conspirators were arrested. Tried at a hastily arranged court martial, they were executed by firing squad the same night in the courtyard of the army headquarters. Stauffenberg was buried immediately, but the next day the SS dug up his body and removed the medals from his uniform. Today, the courtyard where he and others were executed is a memorial site.

Public criticism

During the war years, anyone who spoke out publicly or who demonstrated openly against Nazi policies risked their life. Despite this, some individuals made brave moral choices.

Cardinal Galen

As you discovered in Enquiry 2, the Catholic Bishop of Münster, Cardinal Galen, began to speak out against Nazi racial policies after 1934 (see page 39). During the war, his opposition increased as the crimes of the regime became more apparent. In 1941, Galen delivered three famous sermons denouncing the use of terror by the Gestapo, the taking of Church property and, most famously, the murder of mentally and physically disabled people. From this he gained the nickname the 'Lion of Münster'. The sermons were printed and distributed illegally. Three of the Catholic priests who took part in this were caught and executed in Lübeck. Galen himself survived the war as he was too prominent a figure to be eliminated, but lived under virtual house arrest from 1941 to 1945.

▲ Cardinal Galen

Dietrich Bonhoeffer

Dietrich Bonhoeffer was a Protestant pastor who had opposed the Nazis from the outset in 1933. During the 1930s, he preached against them and trained new pastors to join his cause. In the late 1930s, he secretly joined the German resistance and, despite being hounded by the Gestapo, continued his work. Banned from writing or speaking publicly, he joined the *Abwehr* (military intelligence), which contained a number of army officers who secretly opposed the Nazi regime. As an *Abwehr* agent he learned of the full scale of the Nazi atrocities and this increased his resistance. Under cover, he relayed messages for the underground resistance and helped to organise the escape of Jews to Switzerland. In 1943, he was arrested and held in jail where he preached to inmates. He was killed in Flossenbürg concentration camp in April 1945, two weeks before the end of war.

▲ Dietrich Bonhoeffer

The Rosenstrasse

Saturday 27 February 1943 saw the last 'Action' to round up the remaining Jews of Berlin (see page 89). One group of men was taken to Rosenstrasse 2–4, a building that had been the Welfare Office of the Berlin Jewish community. The Jews taken to Rosenstrasse were those whom the Nazis considered to be 'part-Jewish'. Many of the men had Aryan wives, and it was these women who gathered in the Rosenstrasse that day. The crowd grew and became a spontaneous protest in support of the captured men.

In the following days, there were around 600 women in Rosenstrasse at any one time. They began to shout 'Gebt uns unsere Manner wieder' (Give us our husbands back). Occasionally the women's chanting was interrupted when SS guards threatened to shoot. The women took cover in side streets, but soon returned. For several days they stood, arm in arm, chanting and shouting. Then, on Friday 5 March, the first prisoners were released. The wider deportation of Jews to the death camps continued, but the women on the Rosenstrasse had shown remarkable courage.

▼ A still from the 2003 film, *Rosenstrasse*

Leaflets and postcards

Speaking out against Nazi rule during the war could cost you your life. So too could writing leaflets and postcards criticising the Nazi regime. Yet some courageous people chose to secretly distribute anti-Nazi texts in an effort to alert people to the brutality of Hitler's government.

The White Rose

The White Rose was a group at Munich University centred around Hans and Sophie Scholl. Influenced by the sermons of Galen and having seen the mistreatment of Jews on the Eastern Front during compulsory service, the students decided to produce a series of anti-Nazi leaflets. The first four leaflets were produced between June and July 1942 and were distributed locally to students, encouraging them to resist the Nazis. The fifth leaflet, produced in January 1943, brought them to prominence. Written for a broader audience, it was entitled an 'Appeal to All Germans' and stated 'Hitler cannot win the war. He can only prolong it.' Between 6000 and 9000 leaflets were distributed to nine large cities around Germany.

After the German army had failed at Stalingrad, the group produced a final sixth leaflet, hoping to encourage the German people to resist the Nazis at a time of low morale. On 18 February 1943, the Scholls brought suitcases of leaflets to the university and dropped them in corridors and lecture rooms, and even threw some from a balcony into the atrium below. Unfortunately, this last act was seen by a caretaker who alerted the Gestapo. The Scholls were arrested. Sophie assumed full responsibility to protect the others but in the end most of the prominent members of the group, including both Sophie and Hans, faced the People's Court and execution.

▲ Hans and Sophie Scholl, leaders of the White Rose Group who wrote anti-Nazi leaflets

Otto and Elise Hampel

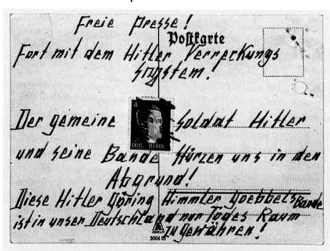

▲ One of the Hampels' postcards. It reads 'Free press! Away with the Hitler dying-a-wretched-death system!' Over Hitler's face on the stamp in the middle are scrawled the words 'worker murderer'.

The Hampels were a working-class couple from Berlin who, although not Nazi supporters, did not readily oppose the regime in its first few years. However, Elise's brother was killed in action in 1940 and it seems that this spurred them into resistance. Between September 1940 and the autumn of 1942, they hand wrote over 200 postcards urging people to refuse military service, to stop donating money to the Nazis and to overthrow Hitler. The postcards were then left in post boxes and stairwells around the Wedding district of Berlin.

Nearly all of the 200 postcards were handed in to the Gestapo, showing the fear the public had of such simple objects of resistance. However, it still took two years to identify the couple. Tried by the People's Court, they were executed in April 1943. Their story was turned into a novel, *Alone in Berlin*, which has been made into a Hollywood film.

Reflect

In what ways had the war motivated the White Rose Group and the Hampels?

Passive resistance from the German population

In the spring of 1943 a Berlin housewife in her mid-forties noticed that the date 1918 had been daubed in paint on a nearby house. It was a simple message which would be immediately understood by everyone who saw it – Germany was once again heading for defeat. The woman was impressed by this simple act of opposition. Early in the morning, when no one would see her, she began writing the date on notices and posters. Whenever she returned to the site of her 'protest' some days later, the date had always been covered in thick black paint. The woman's action was a small act of defiance, for which she could have been executed. She later recalled that she was simply trying to give other Berliners 'a sign of life'.

Writing anti-Nazi graffiti was just one way in which Germans showed their opposition to Nazi rule during the war years. Individual acts of opposition took a variety of forms:

- Saying 'Good morning' instead of *'Heil Hitler'*
- Telling anti-Nazi jokes
- Reading banned literature
- Listening to the BBC
- Hiding Jews

It is difficult to know how much of this 'passive resistance' took place, but historians have concluded that it increased during the war years. As soldiers returned from the Eastern Front, information about the barbaric treatment of Poles and Jews filtered through, and people began to turn against the Nazis. From 1943, the regime took a tougher line when dealing with these trivial offences. For example, in 1944, a Berlin munitions worker was executed for telling the following joke: 'Hitler and Göring are standing on top of Berlin's radio tower. Hitler says he wants to do something to cheer up the people of Berlin. "Why don't you just jump?" suggests Göring.'

Lack of knowledge: Most people had little direct experience of Nazi brutality. It is very difficult to know how much ordinary Germans knew of the Nazi crimes that were taking place in their country and in wider Europe. However, a lot was covered up and many claim they had no idea about events such as the Holocaust.

Fear: The repressive nature of the Nazi regime meant people were scared of stepping out of line. During the war, persecution increased, making opposition even more difficult. People knew what could happen to them if they opposed the Nazis.

Why wasn't there more opposition?

Nazi propaganda: The Nazi propaganda machine became even more effective during the war years. Goebbels and his ministry fought hard to win the hearts and minds of the German people, and sold them the myth that Hitler would be their saviour.

Nazi success: Hitler's foreign policy was successful until 1941. The Nazis also delivered on its promises to protect the German people. There was a massive programme of bunker-building to protect the civilian population. Welfare schemes helped people whose homes were destroyed by Allied bombing. These successes convinced many Germans that the Nazis deserved their support.

Record

Write a planning sheet for the second part of your documentary programme: 'Opposition to the Nazis during the war years'.

Total war, 1943–45

The move to 'total war', 1943

Until 1943, the German war machine had been largely successful. However, in late January of that year, the Nazis faced their first major defeat by the Russians at the Battle of Stalingrad. By the beginning of 1943, the British and French had pushed the Germans out of North Africa. The tide of war was turning.

Goebbels' plan for total war

Faced with these losses, the Nazis needed a new plan. The war could only be won if the German people made huge sacrifices. 'Total war' was now required.

On 18 February 1943, Goebbels addressed a large public meeting at the Berlin Sportpalast. The stadium had once hosted ice-hockey games, but had been used for political rallies since 1933. The Sportpalast had been carefully prepared for Goebbels' speech. Huge swastika banners hung from the balconies. At one end of the stadium there was a long white platform from where Goebbels would speak. The Nazi flag hung in

the centre and a stylised eagle stretched out behind. Above, there was a huge banner with the words 'Total War – Shortest War'.

The crowd in the Sportpalast had been carefully selected from a cross-section of the German people who were loyal Nazis. Goebbels made a long and powerful speech, which was broadcast on German radio. He explained the need for 'total war' and asked his audience a series of questions:

- 'Do you believe with the *Führer* and us in the final total victory of the German people?'
- 'Are you and the German people willing to work, if the *Führer* orders, ten, twelve and if necessary fourteen hours a day and to give everything for victory?'
- 'If necessary, do you want a war more total and radical than anything that we can even imagine today?'

The crowd's response of 'Yes!' became louder with each question.

▲ Goebbels delivering his speech at the Sportpalast, 18 February 1943

The impact on the German people

The move to total war that Goebbels outlined in February 1943 had a drastic impact on the lives of German civilians in the months that followed:

- **The Nazis finally tried to mobilise women into the war effort.** A total of 3 million eligible women between the ages of 17 and 45 were called to work. Only 1 million actually took up the call, with some avoiding it by deliberately getting pregnant.
- **Anything that did not contribute to the war effort was eliminated.** Professional sport was ended, magazines were closed and non-essential businesses were shut down. For example, women could have a haircut but hair dyeing was banned.
- **The shortages became even worse.** In August 1943, clothes rationing was suspended as the production of civilian clothes ended. As an alternative, exchange centres were set up where people could swap unwanted clothes or furniture.
- **There was an increase in propaganda** encouraging people to embrace the idea of total war. Goebbels' speech was shown in cinemas around the country and posters like the one on the right were posted throughout Germany.

The impact of air raids

British and American planes had been bombing German towns and cities since 1940, but in 1943 they intensified their attacks. In late July 1943, the Allies bombed Hamburg in a concentrated series of day and night raids. The air raids on Hamburg's narrow streets of wooden buildings created a firestorm that tore through the city. Half of Hamburg was destroyed and more than 40,000 civilians were killed.

In November 1943, the RAF began an intense attack on the German capital, Berlin. On the night of 22 November, 750 planes attacked the city. Within a week, the Berliners faced four bombing raids, which were more horrific than anything they had experienced before. The city's strong air defences meant that deaths were limited to 3758, but about half a million people were left homeless and nearly 100,000 were injured.

Goebbels had chance to witness the destruction when he left his underground bunker on the evening of 24 November for the safety of his country house to the west of Berlin:

> What I saw was truly shattering. The whole Tiergarten quarter has been destroyed, so has the section around the Zoo. While the outer facades of the great buildings are still standing, everything inside is burnt to the ground … Groups of people scamper across the street like veritable ghosts. How beautiful Berlin was at one time and how run down and woebegone it looks now.

▲ This poster, published in 1943, says 'All power stretched to total war! Shortest war!' Rolling up your sleeves and joining in the war effort was a common theme of propaganda.

Desperation, 1944

In 1944, the war in Europe turned further still against the Nazis. In the spring, the US and Britain continued their air raids on German cities. In June, the Allies successfully invaded northern France and began an assault on northern Europe. By August, they had liberated Paris. In the east, Soviet forces entered Romania and moved into Poland.

1944 brought chaos and confusion to Germany. Continued Allied bombing devastated many cities. People struggled to survive in the ruins. Many fled to seek safety in the countryside. As the Allies and Russians advanced through Nazi-occupied countries, native Germans poured back into their motherland. The huge number of refugees added to the pressures on fuel and food in Germany.

The summer of 1944 saw a huge increase in arrests and executions. The shock of the July bomb plot led to a surge in Hitler's popularity. It also provided an opportunity to bring the people and the army into line. The Gestapo and SS arrested over 7000 people whom they managed to connect to the plot, and they executed 5000 of them. Many of those executed were *Wehrmacht* officers, who were then replaced by Nazi-loyalists. For the first time, the Hitler salute became compulsory in the army.

▼ A fire in central Berlin after an air raid in July 1944

Increasing the war effort

The Nazis knew that in order to have a chance of winning the war they had to continue their push toward total war. In July 1944, Goebbels was made Reich Trustee for Total War, putting him in charge of ensuring that every aspect of German society was working towards the war effort. He immediately increased the pressure on the German people:

- Half a million workers were ordered to become soldiers. Many of these men had worked in arms factories and were replaced with untrained workers. This had a negative impact on production, but the Nazis desperately needed soldiers to fight on the eastern and western fronts.
- The age limit for compulsory service for women was increased to 50.
- There was an increase in forced labour, which had been used in Germany since the start of the war. By the summer of 1944, 7.6 million foreign workers had been brought to Germany, making up a quarter of the workforce.
- To save fuel, railway and postal services were reduced.
- All theatres, opera houses and music halls were closed.
- Propaganda was strengthened still further. Many posters encouraged people to be careful what they said in public.

◀ Propaganda continued to be published in 1944. This poster translates as 'Pst – the enemy listens in!'

The *Volkssturm*

In October 1944, as the military situation worsened for the Nazis, Hitler ordered the creation of the *Volkssturm* (People's Storm). This was a National Militia, which the Nazis hoped would be able to defend Germany against the advancing Russian and Allied troops. All males between the ages of 16 and 60 who were not already in military service were forced to join the *Volkssturm*. Nazi officials even patrolled the wards of German hospitals searching for injured soldiers who were fit enough to hold a gun and could be pressed back into service.

▲ A *Volkssturm* armband

Members of the *Volkssturm* received just four days' training. There were no uniforms. The men were simply ordered to avoid brightly coloured clothing and were given an armband to wear. They were issued with old rifles and captured foreign weapons. The sight of these teenagers and middle-aged men marching through the streets of town and cities can have done little to raise the morale of the German people.

▼ A parade of the *Volkssturm* in Berlin for Goebbels, 12 November 1944

Chaos, destruction and peace, 1945

In early spring 1945, both the British and Americans in the west, and the Soviets in the east, made rapid progress against the Germans. In March, the British and Americans crossed the Rhine into Germany. In April, the Soviets crossed Germany's eastern border. Yet the Germans fought on until all that remained of the Third Reich was a handful of people in Hitler's bunker. On 30 April 1945, realising the end had arrived, Hitler took his own life and a week later the war in Europe was over.

Falling apart

The chaos of the last few months of war was reflected in German society. As the Nazi leadership panicked in the face of inevitable defeat, the infrastructure of the country began to fall apart. Ration cards became useless as the shops ran out of goods. There were severe food shortages. Those with money turned to the black market to survive. Others faced starvation.

British and American bombing became particularly ferocious in the last year of the war. In February 1945, Dresden was bombed in four raids by 727 British planes and 527 American planes. Together they dropped nearly 4000 tons of high explosive on the city. This resulted in a firestorm that destroyed 1600 acres of Dresden and led to the deaths of around 25,000 people. The loss of civilian lives was so high that some people later argued that the British and American officials who ordered the bombing raids should have been put on trial for war crimes.

▼ Dresden after the British and Americans had heavily bombed the city in February 1945. As you can see, much of the city is in ruins. This iconic photo was taken from the top of the remains of the Town Hall with a statue appearing to angelically survey the damage.

Fighting to the bitter end

By April, the empire of the Third Reich had shrunk to Berlin alone. With the Soviet troops surrounding the city by the middle of the month, you would have expected the people and leadership to surrender, but they fought on. With depleted *Wehrmacht* and SS forces, the fight was continued with help from the *Volkssturm* and the Hitler Youth. The latter had become increasingly militarised during the war and now took an active role. Faced with an army of many times their number, defeat was inevitable and, on 2 May, the Germans finally surrendered.

In his 2011 book, the historian Ian Kershaw examined what the last two years of the war meant for the people of Germany. He opens the book *The End* with the following words:

> As disastrous defeat loomed in early 1945, Germans were sometimes heard to say they would prefer 'an end with horror, to a horror without end'. An 'end with horror' was certainly what they experienced, in ways and dimensions unprecedented in history. The end brought destruction and human loss on an immense scale.

In the book Kershaw sought to explain why the Nazi regime was able to hold together when it was under so much pressure in the last two years of the war. He argued that a combination of terror, propaganda and faith in Hitler held the Nazi regime together to the bitter end.

▼ The historian Ian Kershaw

▼ The cover of Ian Kershaw's 2011 book, *The End*

Record

Write a planning sheet for the final part of your documentary programme: 'The move to "total war" in the period 1943–45'.

Review

Decide on an overall title for your TV documentary and plan a three-minute opening sequence.

Berlin and the end of the Third Reich, April 1945

▲ A Russian tank amid the ruins of Berlin, May 1945

At the beginning of 1942, the Third Reich stretched from the outskirts of Moscow to the western coast of France. Three years later, in April 1945, all that remained was the once great city of Berlin. The Nazis were defeated by the Soviets in the east and the Allies in the west, but Berlin fought on.

On 20 April, it was Hitler's birthday. He emerged from the underground bunker in the centre of the city that had become his home since January. Hitler made awards to members of the Hitler Youth for their bravery, still believing that Germany could triumph. He was deluded. The Soviet Red Army had already encircled Berlin in what would become the last great offensive of the Second World War in Europe. That evening, the Soviets began a shelling campaign that lasted for two weeks. Already devastated by British, American and French bombs during the previous four years, Berlin took a final hammering. In the final days of the war, more than 2 million shells landed on the city.

Berlin faced 1.5 million Soviet soldiers and was defended by only 80,000 men. This was not the well-polished *Wehrmacht* of earlier victories, but a hastily-put-together group of those who were left. Half were made up of the *Volkssturm*, with little training and few effective weapons. The other half were regular soldiers, many of whom were tired and broken from six years of war. It is not surprising that they were crushed by the Soviets.

While German troops fought on the streets of the city, the citizens of Berlin hid in cellars or bunkers, often with no toilet facilities and limited food supplies. Those who were brave enough to venture outside found a scene of devastation and danger. One Berliner, Ruth Andreas-Friedrich, wrote:

No express trains are moving in or out. All transportation is at a standstill. Postal and telegraph services have ceased. We are cut off from the world, for better or worse, at the mercy of the oncoming catastrophe.

The people of Berlin were in great fear of what would happen when the city finally fell to Soviet forces. Thousands of people took their own lives.

On 30 April, Hitler faced the reality that he had refused to accept in the previous weeks: this was the end. A few hours after marrying his partner Eva Braun, they both committed suicide by swallowing cyanide capsules and then shooting themselves with pistols. The Third Reich was over. By 2 May, the Reichstag had been captured by Soviet troops and the fighting had ended. On 9 May, victory was claimed by the Allies and a peace was signed in the outskirts of Berlin.

For the people of Berlin the nightmare was not over. Four years of bombing and two weeks of intensive shelling meant that hundreds of thousands of families had lost their homes and were reduced to living in the rubble of the city. Food supplies were dangerously low and people feared starvation. Some even butchered the dead animals in the street to survive. It was the women of Berlin who had most to fear from the Soviet invasion. Hospital records reveal that between 90,000 and 130,000 women were raped in the weeks after the surrender. Many other rapes went unregistered. The horror of these last few weeks of the war would never be forgotten by the people of Berlin.

▲ Members of the *Volkssturm* with bazookas, ready to defend the city, Berlin, 1945

▼ Berliners butchering a dead horse on the street, 1945

5

Occupation

What did Nazi rule mean for the people of Europe, 1939–45?

▲ A British policeman and a German air force officer in St Helier, the capital of Jersey, summer 1940

At first sight, this is a surprising photograph. It shows a German air force officer talking to a British policeman in the summer of 1940. As you know, Germany never managed to invade Britain during the Second World War, but the Nazis did succeed in occupying one part of the British Isles – the Channel Islands. On 30 June 1940, German forces landed, unopposed, on the two main islands of Jersey and Guernsey. The occupation lasted for nearly five years until the Channel Islands were finally liberated on 9 May 1945.

Following their invasion in 1940, the Nazis quickly took control. All laws had to be approved by the German *kommandant* but the Channel Island politicians were allowed to remain in post in order to assist with the smooth running of the occupation. The politicians were faced with difficult decisions. They felt that they had to co-operate but did not want to be seen as collaborators.

For the people of the Channel Islands, resistance was difficult. Most of the men on the islands were away serving in the British army. It was the women who remained, with the young and elderly men. On such small islands, armed resistance and sabotage were impossible, but people made their own moral choices about how far they co-operated with the occupation. At the extremes, some women had relationships with German soldiers, while others risked their lives by printing underground newspapers. Many people tried to undermine the occupation by breaking the rules, refusing to speak to the Germans or writing anti-Nazi graffiti. From a population of 66,000 during the war, 4000 Channel Islanders were sentenced for breaking the law, and 570 of these were imprisoned.

In October 1941, Hitler announced that the Channel Islands would become an 'impregnable fortress' as part of the Atlantic Wall of fortifications that he planned for the entire coast of western Europe. Massive gun emplacements, underground bunkers and tunnels were built along the coast of the Islands. Most Channel Islanders refused to help in the construction so slave labour was brought from Nazi territory in eastern Europe. Four concentration camps were built on Alderney to house over 16,000 prisoners who were brought to the island during the years of occupation. Around 700 died due to the harsh treatment received in the Nazi slave labour camps on Alderney.

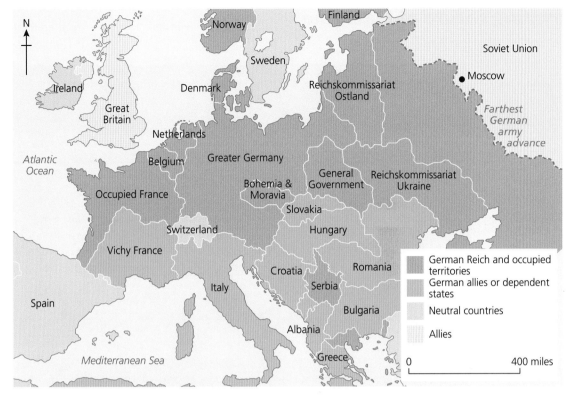

▲ Europe in 1942 at the height of Nazi control

This map shows the Nazi occupation of Europe when it was at its greatest extent in 1942. As you can see, by 1942 the Third Reich stretched to the Atlantic Ocean in the west and had almost reached Moscow in the east.

Reflect

Look at the map. Which present-day countries were under Nazi occupation?

The Enquiry

Nazi occupation varied from country to country, and within each country people were affected in different ways. In this enquiry, you will build your knowledge of what happened during the Nazi occupation of Europe and analyse what Nazi rule meant for different people. You will do this in three stages:

1. You will begin by analysing the contrasting nature of Nazi rule in eastern and western Europe. Your focus will be on the occupations of Poland and the Netherlands. You will complete a Venn diagram to analyse the similarities and differences between the occupation of the two countries.
2. You will then investigate how and why the Nazi regime murdered 6 million European Jews in the most disturbing event of Europe's history – the Holocaust. You will produce clear summaries of the different aspects of the Holocaust to analyse this complex and horrific aspect of Nazi occupation.
3. Finally, you will examine how people reacted to Nazi rule across Europe. To consider different reactions, you will decide where to place selected people and groups on a continuum line from collaboration to resistance.

The contrasting nature of Nazi rule in eastern and western Europe

As you discovered from the map on page 81, the Nazis occupied a number of countries across Europe. They treated each country differently, but overall the occupation in the east was very different from the occupation of western Europe. We can explore this by focusing on two examples: the occupation of Poland (in the east) and the Netherlands (in the west).

Record

As you read pages 82–83, make a list of the main features of the Nazi occupation of Poland.

▶ The *Wehrmacht* marching through Warsaw in 1939

The occupation of Poland

Poland had only officially existed as a country since the end of the First World War in 1918. Before this, in the nineteenth century, it had been part of an area controlled by Germany. Nazi leaders, who believed that Germany needed *Lebensraum*, saw it as their right to take back what they believed belonged to Germany. When the Nazis invaded Poland in September 1939, they aimed to remove any element of Polish control or culture. Their plan was to totally Germanise the country.

By October 1939, Poland had ceased to exist. Nazi leaders split the country into different regions and incorporated some into existing German territories. The fifth and largest region was named General Government. There was discussion as to whether the name should be General Government of Poland, but the Nazis decided to remove all trace of the country.

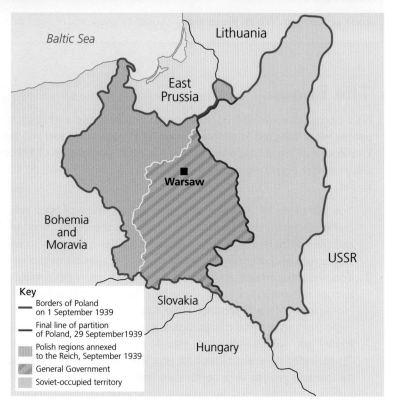

▶ The German occupation of Poland, 1939

Key
— Borders of Poland on 1 September 1939
— Final line of partition of Poland, 29 September 1939
Polish regions annexed to the Reich, September 1939
General Government
Soviet-occupied territory

The removal of Polish culture and people

In 1940, Himmler drew up his Eastern General Plan, a strategy for occupation in the east which would be tested in Poland. The plan was simple – to remove as many of the Polish or Slavic people as possible and to replace them with Germans. From 1940, hundreds of thousands of native Polish citizens were expelled, and 500,000 'ethnic Germans' were settled in their houses and on their lands.

Many of the native Poles were moved into the General Government region. This was governed by Hans Frank, a Nazi ex-lawyer, who introduced a rule of terror. In May 1940, Frank destroyed Polish culture, education and leadership. Schools and universities were closed. Polish intellectuals and political leaders were particularly targeted. Around 30,000 of the most talented people in Poland were arrested. Many were tortured and murdered.

The Nazis considered Slavic Poles to be racially inferior and, from the outset, large numbers were murdered by the *Wehrmacht* and the SS. It is estimated that 1.9 million non-Jewish citizens were killed. Other Poles were sent to work in Germany through forced labour schemes. Between 1939 and 1945, over 1.5 million were deported and forced to work in labour camps. In May 1940, the Polish Decrees established rules for Poles working in Germany. All were forced to wear a P on their arm, humiliating them and singling them out as different. Sexual relations with Germans were banned and a lower wage than that paid to German workers was enforced.

▲ Hans Frank, Governor General of Poland

Things were even worse for Polish Jews. From the outset, they experienced persecution and brutality. From 1940, Jews were concentrated in ghettos (see page 87). The Jewish population of Poland in 1939 was roughly 3.5 million. Before the end of the war, the Nazis had murdered over 3 million Polish Jews. In order to do this, a network of concentration camps and death camps (the sole function of which was murder) was established throughout Poland (see page 89).

Resistance

The Nazis' destruction of Poland, and the brutality of their occupation, led the Polish people to form one of the largest and most complex resistance movements in the whole of Nazi-occupied Europe.

▲ A memorial to murdered Polish victims at Poliak prison in Warsaw. Many leaders were sent here, tortured and executed

The Polish government, which had escaped to London in 1939, helped to establish Delegatura, a secret state within Poland. In August 1944, the Poles staged an uprising in Warsaw, a bitter struggle against Nazi rule that lasted for two months. In the end, the uprising was brutally crushed by the Nazis. Hitler ordered the complete destruction of Warsaw and its people. Patients in a city hospital were even shot as they lay in their beds. In total, 200,000 people were killed and the city of Warsaw was completely destroyed.

Reflect

Compare your list of the main features of the Nazi occupation of Poland with a partner. Do you need to change or add anything?

The occupation of the Netherlands

▲ Rotterdam, following the air raid on 14 May 1940

German troops invaded the Netherlands on 10 May 1940. After four days of fighting on the ground, the *Luftwaffe* attacked. On 14 May, Rotterdam, an important trading city with a large dock, was heavily bombed. Over 800 people were killed and 25,000 homes were destroyed as the *Luftwaffe* targeted civilian areas.

Fearing similar destruction and loss of life in other cities, the Dutch government surrendered. Five years of Nazi occupation began in the Netherlands.

The Dutch royal family and government refused to co-operate with the Nazi invaders, and escaped to exile in the UK. As a result, the Netherlands was put under the control of Arthur Seyss-Inquart, an Austrian Nazi. Democracy was abolished and parliament dissolved.

The occupation begins, 1940

The Dutch shared the same ethnic background as Germans and were therefore treated very differently from the Slavs of the east. Civil servants were allowed to continue working if they chose to, although 30 per cent of town mayors stepped down. The Dutch education system was not changed as the Nazi rulers realised there would be a backlash if they tried to interfere.

The Dutch were known to respect authority and at first there was general compliance with Nazi regulations. In October 1940, when civil servants were forced to complete ancestry forms to remove 'Jewish elements', nearly everyone filled in the forms. Nevertheless, from the outset, the Dutch found small ways to resist Nazi rule. On 29 June 1940, Prince Bernhard's birthday, many Dutch citizens wore carnations in support of the royal family in exile. The Germans reacted by removing royal portraits and changing royal street names, but no one was punished for their resistance.

▶ A recruitment poster to get Dutch men to join the SS reads 'Your place is still vacant in the Waffen-SS'.

The turning point, 1941–42

In 1941, the nature of Nazi rule in the Netherlands began to change. In February, the first Jewish men (425 of them) were rounded up for deportation. Dutch communists called for a strike in retaliation. Trams stopped working and strikers marched in the streets in many Dutch towns. The Germans abandoned their 'friendly' attitude and shot at the strikers. Nine were killed and hundreds arrested. On 13 March, the first death sentences against Dutch citizens were issued. Three strikers and fifteen members of the Dutch resistance were shot. The strike and the German reaction strengthened the mood of Dutch people against the Nazi occupiers.

Intimidation and violence, 1943–44

In 1943, the Germans abandoned their attempts to win over the Dutch and switched to intimidation and violence. The 140,000 Jews living in the Netherlands were their main target. Already, by April 1942, all Jews had to wear the Star of David. In 1943, the Nazis began deporting Jews to extermination camps in huge numbers. In all, 107,000 Jews (76 per cent of the total Jewish population of the Netherlands) were deported. This was partly due to Dutch compliance but also more to do with the difficulty of hiding people in a small and densely populated country.

By 1943, with so many German men fighting on the front lines, there was a severe shortage of workers in Germany. In April, it was announced that 300,000 Dutch ex-soldiers would be transported to Germany to work as forced labourers. Strikes erupted across the country. The brutal Nazi response resulted in 95 people being killed and 400 wounded. By late May, all Dutch men between the ages of 18 and 35 were to become forced labourers. Of the 170,000 who were expected to report for duty, only 54,000 did so. By 1944, all men between the ages of 16 and 60 had to report for forced labour and 500,000 ended up working in Germany, a third of all eligible men.

As a result of this oppression, Dutch resistance developed as men hid from forced labour and joined the forces resisting Nazi rule. By 1944, there were 300,000 men in hiding. Many illegal printing presses were established, producing anti-Nazi leaflets which encouraged more people to resist forced labour. Armed resistance began as registry offices were attacked for ration coupons and blank identity cards. Almost 20,000 resistance members were arrested. Most were sent to the four Dutch concentration camps but others were imprisoned in Germany. Around 2000 members of the Dutch resistance were executed.

▼ Resistance groups were increasingly ingenious in their techniques. This hollow chessboard was used by the Westerweel Group to hide false documents. Set up by teacher Joop Westerweel, the group managed to help 150 Jews escape.

The beginning of the end, late 1944

Realising the end of occupation was near, in September 1944, the Dutch government in exile called for railway strikes. As a result, 30,000 rail workers went into hiding. The Germans found their own trains to use but with fewer Dutch trains there was a severe lack of transport. Coal and food were in short supply. Living conditions had slowly worsened through the war but in the winter of 1944–45 food shortages became severe. In the final years of the war, 20,000 Dutch people died of starvation.

On 5 May 1945, five years of Nazi occupation came to an end when the Netherlands was liberated by Canadian soldiers.

▲ Food shortages became so severe that some families like the Bontekoe family received parcels of potatoes from their relatives who were farmers.

Record

Now use your two lists to complete a Venn diagram comparing the Nazi occupation of Poland and the Netherlands.

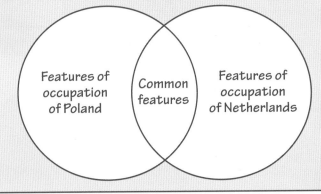

Features of occupation of Poland

Common features

Features of occupation of Netherlands

The Holocaust

By the time the Second World War ended in 1945, the Nazis had murdered 11 million individuals, including Jews, Slavs, Gypsies, communists and homosexuals. Of these 11 million, nearly 6 million were Jewish people whom the Nazis had decided to systematically eradicate. This crime is called the Holocaust.

In 1939, the Jewish population of Europe was 9.5 million. Jewish communities were found in many parts of the continent, but there was a heavy concentration of Jews in the east. As the Nazis began to occupy other European countries they controlled a far larger population of Jews. To the Nazis this was a 'Jewish problem' that needed a solution.

Record

As you learn about the Holocaust, produce a series of small cards to sum up the different stages.

▲ Jews being forced to scrub the pavements in Vienna. Austrians stood by and watched. Around the world, newspapers shared these horrific scenes of humiliation.

The first solution: persecution and emigration (1938–39)

In the countries the Nazis occupied before the start of the Second World War, the first solution was to force Jews to leave the country. This policy was adopted in Austria following the Nazi invasion in March 1938. At that time, Austria had a Jewish population of 192,000, with 167,000 Jews in Vienna alone. Before March 1938, Jews had equal status with other Austrian citizens, but this changed as soon as the Nazi occupation began. Jews were beaten and humiliated by being forced to scrub the pavements to get rid of pro-Austrian graffiti. At the same time, mass looting or 'Aryanisation' of property began, initially by individuals but soon organised by the SS, who took expensive belongings and, often, whole properties.

The persecution led many Jews to consider emigration. This was actively encouraged by the Nazis, who created a Central Office for Jewish Emigration. According to official reports, 110,000 Jews emigrated in two years. The 'Vienna Model', combining persecution and encouraged emigration, had been quickly established. It was a model that would be repeated in Czechoslovakia the following year.

Record

Produce your first information card on 'Emigration, 1938–39'.

Maria Altmann's story

Sometimes it takes a long time to get justice. Maria was one of the 110,000 Jews who were forced to emigrate from Vienna in 1938. Like many wealthy Jews, she was forced to leave behind many of her treasured possessions. One of these was her favourite portrait of her aunt by the famous artist Gustav Klimt. Maria had always assumed that her uncle had given the painting to the state museum. Then, in 1998, a journalist discovered it had been looted by the Nazis and should have been left to Maria. In 2000, she took the Austrian government to court. Sixty-two years after it was stolen, the portrait was returned to its rightful owner.

▲ Maria Altmann and her painting

The second solution: concentration in ghettos (1939–41)

In September 1939, when the Nazis invaded Poland, the scale and nature of the 'Jewish problem' changed. Emigration could not be an effective solution in a country with 3.5 million Jews. A new solution was needed. A plan was formed to move all the Jews of Europe to a reservation (areas in the Soviet Union and Madagascar were discussed), but in 1940 the Nazis did not own an area of land where such a reservation was possible. Instead, Polish Jews (and soon others from other countries) were concentrated into ghettos so they would be ready for a mass deportation once a suitable reservation was found.

Ghettos were enclosed districts that isolated Jews by separating Jewish communities from the non-Jewish population. They varied in size and there were hundreds in German-occupied Poland alone. The largest ghetto in Nazi-occupied Poland was in Warsaw. Completed in November 1940, the ghetto had three-metre-high walls topped with barbed wire. By March 1941, the Warsaw Ghetto held 445,000 Jewish inhabitants. This was a third of the city's population, in just 2.4 per cent of its area. On average, fifteen people shared a small apartment. Unsurprisingly, these conditions led to disease and death, particularly among the vulnerable, like the young and old. In the autumn of 1941 alone, there were 900 cases of typhus (a bacterial infection with severe flu-like symptoms which is often fatal) in the Warsaw Ghetto. In its three-year existence, over 140,000 died here. High death rates were common in ghettos across eastern Europe.

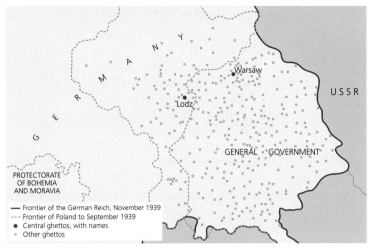

▲ Ghettos in Nazi-occupied Poland

Frontier of the German Reich, November 1939
Frontier of Poland to September 1939
● Central ghettos, with names
▪ Other ghettos

▲ A Jewish boy being searched for smuggled goods in the Warsaw Ghetto

Emanuel Ringelblum's story

Emanuel Ringelblum was a Polish–Jewish historian, teacher and political activist. In 1940, he and his family were forced into the Warsaw Ghetto. Realising that no one would have an accurate account of the lives of Polish Jews during the German occupation, Ringelblum decided to form a collection of documents as a testimony for future generations. At great risk, he formed a secret organisation, which began collecting diaries, papers and posters from people in the ghetto. Before the Nazis destroyed the Warsaw Ghetto, the organisation hid the archive in three metal milk cans and ten metal boxes. Emanuel Ringelblum and his family were murdered by the Gestapo but, after the war, some of the boxes and milk cans were discovered under the ruins of Warsaw. The Ringelblum Archive preserves a powerful memory of the suffering and resilience of the Jewish people in Poland.

◁ Emanuel Ringelblum

The final solution: murder (1941–45)

Phase one: the *Einsatzgruppen*

The mass murder of Jews began with the Nazi invasion of the Soviet Union in June 1941. For the Nazis, this was a life-and-death struggle against communists and Jews in the east. The invading forces were given orders to purge the Soviet-occupied territories of all 'hostile elements'. Jews in particular were to be targeted.

The men who carried out the mass murders in the east belonged to the *Einsatzgruppen*. These were mobile killing units, which consisted of SS men as well as police and auxiliary units recruited from the local population. Four *Einsatzgruppen* (A, B, C and D), each consisting of 500–1000 men, followed the German fighting troops as they advanced into Russian-held territory.

As they reached different villages and towns, the *Einsatzgruppen* rounded up Jews and communists. Men, women and children were taken to secluded areas, often in woodland. There, the victims were forced to dig a large pit. They were then lined up at the edge of the pit and shot. Approximately 90 per cent of those murdered in the autumn and winter of 1941 were Jews, around 1 million people.

▶ This map was part of a report delivered by SS Brigadier Stahlecker entitled 'Jewish Executions Carried out by *Einsatzgruppen* A'

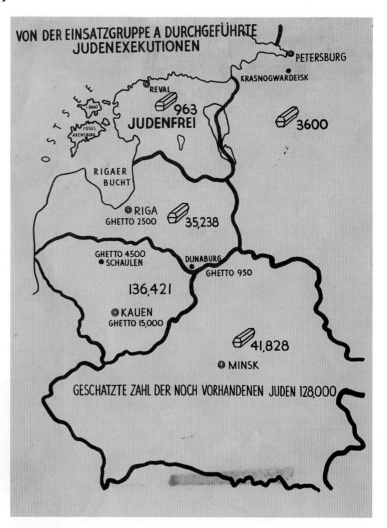

Reflect

What can this source tell us about Nazi killings on the Eastern Front in 1941?

Dina Pronicheva's story

On 29 September 1941, the Jewish population of Kiev, Ukraine, was assembled. Among them was Dina Pronicheva, a Jewish actress from the city. They had been told by the Nazi invaders that they were to be 'resettled'. Marched a few miles outside the city limits, the Jews arrived at Babi Yar ravine, which was 150 metres long, 30 metres wide and 15 metres deep. In small groups, the Jews were led into the ravine and forced to lie down, before machine guns were fired upon them. Dina was one of the last to face this fate. She escaped the bullets and played dead even as soil was poured on top of the bodies to cover the massacre. Later, she dug her way out through the bodies and dirt and managed to survive the war; 33,701 other Jews did not. Babi Yar was one of the largest mass murders in the history of the Second World War.

▷ Dina Pronicheva was a witness at the Kiev war-crimes trials in 1946.

Phase two: death by gas

While the Jews on the Eastern Front were killed with bullets, a different method was being used in German-occupied Poland. At Chelmno, a camp 30 miles north of the Polish town of Łódź, Jews were being murdered by exhaust fumes in vans, a method that allowed greater numbers to be killed and had less of a negative psychological impact on the SS soldiers doing the killing. With no obvious reservation for the concentrated Jews in the ghettos, this provided a solution. The Jews of German-occupied Poland would not be resettled; they would be murdered.

In the autumn of 1941, Operation Reinhard, the extermination of all the Jews in the General Government, was agreed. New extermination or death camps were created, the sole purpose of which was to murder. By 1942, Belzec (March), Sobibor (May) and Treblinka (July) were all operational, murdering Jews in newly constructed gas chambers.

Each of these camps was kept in great secrecy. Managed by only 20 to 35 officers, the camps were all in wooded areas away from large towns. Jews were deported from the ghettos and would arrive at what appeared to be a train station. They were then stripped of their clothing and possessions before being gassed in chambers, which had been made to look like showers. Afterwards Jewish slave labourers would remove the bodies, which were either buried or burnt.

To stop mass panic during this process, Jews were tricked into thinking that they were being resettled in the east. However, rumours soon began to spread in the ghettos and it became apparent to many what was happening. It is remarkable that some Jews managed to resist the process. At Sobibor in 1944, Jews rose up and managed to kill eleven SS guards, allowing 300 Jews to escape. But isolated acts of resistance could not stop the Holocaust in Poland. By the end of the war, 1.7 million Polish Jews had been murdered in Nazi death camps.

▼ The main deportations and death camps, 1942–44

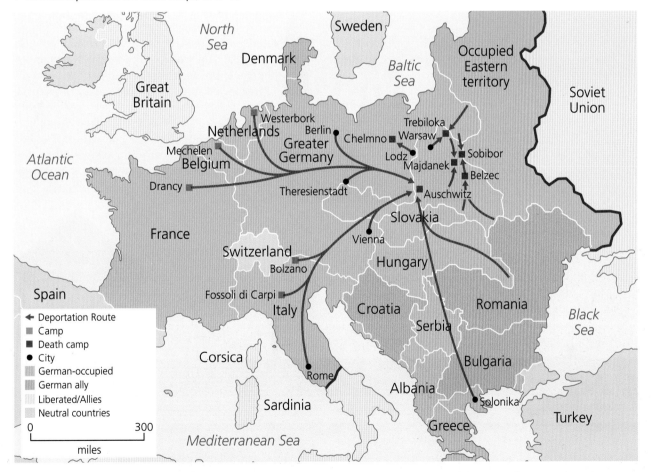

Record

Produce more summary cards to explain the different phases of the Holocaust.

On 20 January 1942, fifteen senior Nazi ministers, led by Reinhard Heydrich, sat down for a lunch meeting at Wannsee, an elegant country house outside Berlin. At the 90-minute meeting, later known as the Wannsee Conference, Heydrich laid out his plans for the mass murder of the Jewish people. The Jews of occupied Europe would be removed from their home countries and transported in trains to the General Government where they would be murdered by gassing. The plans were meticulously detailed and included the exact numbers of Jews in each country, even those they had not yet occupied, such as Great Britain. Adolf Eichmann, a senior SS officer who was at the meeting, was put in charge of organising this mass murder.

Auschwitz: the death factory

After the invasion of Poland, a number of concentration camps were constructed across the country including, in October 1940, one outside the village of Oświęcim, which had the German name Auschwitz. It was in this camp that experiments to mass murder prisoners using Zyklon B, a gas used to kill rodents, began in September 1941. This proved to be highly effective. By late 1941, Auschwitz I was overrun with prisoners and a second site, Auschwitz II-Birkenau, was created. It was this site that was chosen by the Nazis as an extermination camp to murder the Jews of Europe. Four gas chambers and crematoria were designed and built to kill and dispose of thousands of Jews at the same time.

Jews from across Europe were transported to the site in cattle trucks. Packed in like animals, with no water or toilet facilities, they endured journeys that sometimes took days.

▲ SS guards perform a selection on the platform at Auschwitz in the summer of 1944

When the trains arrived at Auschwitz, the prisoners formed two lines of men and women. SS guards and doctors then began a selection process. The fit and able were sent to the right to work as slaves in the factories connected to the site. Everyone else (about three-quarters of those who arrived) was sent to the left to be gassed immediately.

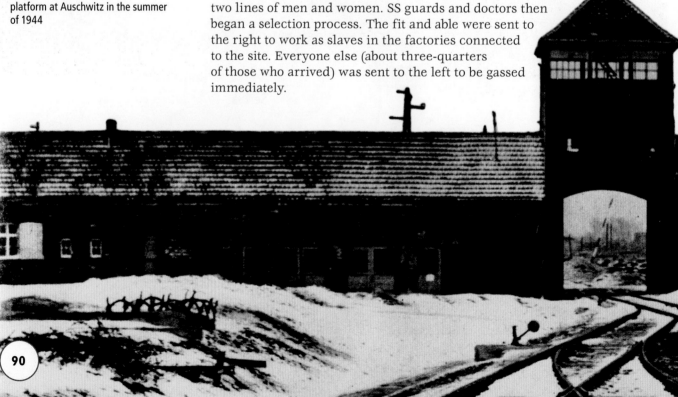

Those sent to the left at the selection were told to undress for a shower and were then led into the gas chamber, which had been designed to look like a shower facility. After the doors were shut, the Zyklon B pellets were dumped through vents in the roof or wall. The victims were dead within twenty minutes. *Sonderkommando*, groups of Jews forced to work for the Nazis, would then enter the chambers, wearing gas masks, and remove the bodies to be burnt in the giant ovens.

At its height, this industrial murder process was killing 12,000 individuals per day. It is estimated that 1.1 million people were murdered at Auschwitz. In total, one in six Holocaust victims was murdered at the site. By nation, the greatest number of Auschwitz's victims were Hungarians. Approximately 438,000 Hungarian Jews were murdered here, half the pre-war Jewish population of the country.

In November 1944, with the Soviet army approaching, Himmler ordered that the gas chambers should be destroyed. In January 1945, the camp was evacuated and 58,000 detainees were put on a death march towards the German border. Thousands died en route, but 20,000 of these individuals were liberated from Bergen-Belsen by the British in April 1945. Those too weak or sick to march, who had been left at the camp, were liberated by the Soviets in late January.

Zigi Shipper's story

In 1940, a ten-year-old Polish Jewish boy called Zigi Shipper was forced into the ghetto which the Nazis had built in the city of Łódź. Two years later, the Nazis rounded up all the children, elderly and disabled people in the Łódź Ghetto, put them onto lorries and deported them to death camps. Zigi managed to escape by jumping from the lorry. He returned to the ghetto where he found work in the metal factory. In 1944, the Nazis liquidated the Łódź Ghetto. Zigi and the other Jews who remained were put in railway cattle trucks and taken to Auschwitz-Birkenau. On arrival, SS guards selected those fit to work (including Zigi) and sent the others to be murdered in the gas chambers. Zigi worked for a few weeks at Auschwitz-Birenau and was then moved to another concentration camp with the other metal workers from Łódź. He was liberated by British troops in May 1945. Two years later, Zigi moved to the UK where he married and had a family. In later life, he helped to educate young people about the Holocaust by sharing his experiences.

▲ Holocaust survivor Zigi Shipper speaking about his experiences, May 2012

▼ The entrance to Auschwitz-Birkenau, 1945

Record

Complete your summary cards explaining the different phases of the Holocaust.

Many people who have not studied the Holocaust in depth only know that the Nazis murdered millions of Jews in Auschwitz. What would you tell these people to help them to understand the complexity of the Holocaust?

Responses to Nazi rule: collaboration, accommodation and resistance

On Monday 3 June 1940, German bombs fell on Paris for the first time since the start of the war. The people of Paris feared that German soldiers would soon be marching into their city. Hundreds of thousands of families, like the one in this photograph, decided to flee.

Reflect

What does the photograph tell us about this family's situation in 1940?

On 20 June, France was defeated by Germany. It was divided into an 'occupied zone' in the north and a 'free zone' in the south. The 'southern zone', known as Vichy France, was ruled by the 84-year-old, right-wing French nationalist, Philippe Pétain.

Nazi occupation in the north brought hardship and suffering to many French families. People felt angry and humiliated to see swastika flags draped over public buildings. German soldiers plundered large quantities of food and other supplies, causing severe shortages. There was strict censorship and a night curfew in the occupied zone. Hundreds of thousands of French workers were taken to Germany as forced labourer. Many men refused to leave France and had to go into hiding. After 1942, over 70,000 French Jews were deported to death camps.

▲ A French family fleeing Paris with the grandmother in a pram, June 1940

Although most people in France did not take part in active resistance against the Nazi occupation, many people engaged in minor acts of resistance such as listening to the BBC on the radio or helping members of the Resistance. Life in occupied France was very dangerous for those who actively resisted Nazi rule. For these people, the Nazis built an execution chamber in the basement of the former Ministry of Aviation building in Paris.

Record

In this section you will learn about the diversity of responses to Nazi rule in France and across occupied Europe. For people at the time there were three options:

- **Collaboration** – working with the Nazis and helping them to rule
- **Accommodation** – doing as you were told by the Nazis
- **Resistance** – opposing the Nazis.

In reality, the lines between these options were blurred and it is better to see this as a continuum line from extreme collaboration to extreme resistance, with accommodation in the middle. Somewhere in the middle is probably where most of us would have been. For each person who lived under Nazi occupation, deciding how to respond often involved difficult moral choices.

On the following three pages are examples of how some individuals and groups responded to Nazi rule. As you read about them, plot each example on a continuum line from Collaboration to Resistance. It would be good to 'pencil in' your decisions at first so that you can decide on the final positions when you have studied the complete range of responses.

Collaboration   Accommodation   Resistance

Two contrasting responses to the occupation of France

We will begin by focusing on two contrasting individuals from France: André Trocmé, living in Vichy France, and Coco Chanel, living in occupied Paris.

André Trocmé

André Trocmé was a Protestant pastor of the small village of Chambon-sur-Lignon in south-east France. A long history of persecution in Catholic France had given the Protestant villagers a dislike for authority. When Vichy France was established, they refused to read the oath to Pétain or to ring the church bells in his honour. Trocmé was a pacifist and cared deeply about all human beings, whatever their religion. When the authorities in Vichy France began putting foreign Jews into concentration camps, he felt that he had to act.

Between December 1940 and September 1944, Trocmé arranged for Jews, mainly children, to be hidden in the region around Chambon-sur-Lignon. The local population worked together to place them in homes, hotels, farms and schools. They forged identification cards, ration cards and, in some cases, led escapes to Switzerland. Whenever they heard that the Vichy police or German security were coming, the inhabitants moved the Jews into the mountains.

In February 1943, Trocmé was arrested. Eventually released after 28 days due to a lack of evidence, he continued his work. But, in late 1943, he had to go into hiding himself for the rest of the war due to fear of further arrest. Although some German raids in the region were successful (in June 1943, they deported five children to Auschwitz), by the time Chambon-sur-Lignon was liberated in September 1944, Trocmé and the other villagers had saved 5000 Jews.

▲ André Trocmé

Coco Chanel

In the 1930s, Coco Chanel had established herself as a very famous fashion designer and perfume maker. In 1940, when the Nazis occupied Paris, wealthy French celebrities like Chanel had the opportunity to stay or leave. Chanel stayed and soon became friends with the Nazi occupiers. Living at the Hotel Ritz, where many prominent German officers stayed, she began a romance with Baron Hans Gunther von Dincklage, a military intelligence officer. In 1941, taking advantage of new anti-Semitic legislation, she tried to persuade the authorities to remove the Jewish directors of her perfume company and give her the sole ownership as an Aryan. In the end this did not happen, but her action revealed her motivation.

In recent years, people have questioned whether Chanel was just a Nazi sympathiser or whether she was working as a Nazi agent. In 2011, historian Hal Vaughan claimed to have found evidence to prove that Chanel was a German spy. He argued that through Dincklage she had met Himmler and forged a plan to write to her friend Winston Churchill to try to negotiate a peace through the SS. Although some refute this, there is growing evidence to suggest that Chanel had a more active role during these war years. After the war she was questioned by the Allied authorities, but lack of evidence, and support from Winston Churchill, meant that she was not convicted.

▲ Coco Chanel in 1929

Reflect

What do you think we can say for certain about the actions of André Trocmé and Coco Chanel?

Record

Decide where to place André Trocmé and Coco Chanel on your continuum line and write a short explanation for each.

Responses to Nazi rule across the rest of Europe

Individuals and groups responded in different ways to Nazi occupation. At one extreme were collaborators who supported Nazi rule. At the other extreme were those who risked their lives to resist the occupation. Of course, most people were in the grey area between collaboration and resistance. They simply 'accommodated' the Nazi occupation and got on with their lives. As a result, we know relatively little about their response. The labels on the map cover a range of responses from different groups across Nazi-occupied Europe, but they are mostly at the extremes of collaboration and resistance.

The Danish people were allowed to keep their government during the war in return for establishing favourable relations with the Germans. Industrial production and trade in Denmark was redirected towards Germany. In return, the Danes were able to reject German demands for legislation against their Jewish population.

Record

Decide where to place each group on your continuum line. Write the name of the group and a note to summarise what it did.

In Belgium, the DeVlag movement was a nationalist group who wanted stronger ties with Nazi Germany. The movement had 50,000 members by 1943. They helped the Nazis to recruit members to the Waffen-SS.

The 'French Resistance' was the term used for the collection of resistance groups in France. They undertook guerrilla warfare against the Nazis, publishing underground newspapers and providing intelligence to the Allies. In June 1944, the military elements formed into the French Interior Force, which helped the Allies push the Nazis out of France.

The Chetniks were a group of Serbian nationalists. In 1943, they agreed to work with the Nazi forces that had invaded Yugoslavia.

During the occupation of Monaco, the police turned over 42 foreign Jewish refugees but protected Monaco's own Jews.

The Ustasa, an extreme right-wing political party in Croatia, were inspired and encouraged by the Nazis to build their own concentration camps, where they killed 25,000 Jews.

Atlantic Ocean · Norway · Denmark · Netherlands · Belgium · Greater German · Bohemi Morav · Switzerland · Italy · Spain · Mediterranean Sea

94

Soviet Union

In Latvia, the SS created the Latvian Auxiliary Security Police or *Arājs Kommando*. The group was composed of students and former army officers with right-wing politics who all volunteered for the job. The *Arājs Kommando* took up the job of purging 'internal enemies' by killing Jews and Communists. The group alone murdered 26,000 Jews, half the Jewish population of Latvia.

Reichskommissariat Ostland

Farthest German army advance

The Bielski partisans were led by four brothers who managed to escape the local Jewish ghetto in Poland and live in the forest. Hundreds of men, women and children joined them and, at its peak, the group numbered 1236. The Bielski partisans lasted two years in the forest, completing numerous sabotage missions against the Nazi rulers.

General Government

Reichskommissariat Ukraine

Significant numbers of Poles helped to rescue an estimated 450,000 Jews from certain death. Aided by the Polish Underground State, they hid and fed Jews to keep them safe from the fate of the Holocaust.

Record

Between pages 80 and 91 there are lots of other examples of collaboration, accommodation and resistance. Re-read these pages and add other groups to your continuum line.

vakia

Hungary

Romania

Serbia

During the occupation of Greece, three Greek prime ministers, chosen and controlled by the Nazis, passed legislation demanded by the occupiers. This included the creation of a 22,000-strong Security Battalion that persecuted the Greek communists.

 German Reich and occupied territories

 German allies or dependent states

Neutral countries

Allies

Greece

ar

0   400 miles

A historian's work on the Holocaust in Hungary

You might think that with so many books, films and television series on the subject, we know everything there is to know about the Nazis. However, historians are still making discoveries about this period. One of these historians is Tim Cole, who is a professor at the University of Bristol and whose work focuses on the Holocaust in Hungary.

In the last enquiry, you found out about the general experience of most Jews in Europe. However, the story of the Holocaust was not the same in every country. The Holocaust in Hungary was quite unusual as ghettoisation and deportation happened at a very late stage in the war and occurred at remarkable speed.

Hungary's war

During the Second World War, Hungary fought on the side of Nazi Germany. It had a right-wing nationalist government like Germany and in the late 1930s passed anti-Semitic legislation, but refused to deport its Jews. This changed when the Nazis, who had become frustrated with the Hungarian government, occupied the country in March 1944. In just over eight weeks, the Jews of Hungary had been ghettoised and the first Jews had been deported. Within another eight weeks, the last deportation took place. In a little over 100 days, 430,000 Hungarian Jews had been deported to the death camps.

▲ Historian, Tim Cole

Tim's research

Tim has explained that he wanted to do something 'from the bottom-up about the experiences of ordinary men and women caught up in the events of 1944' as this reflected his interest 'in the lives of ordinary men and women in extraordinary circumstances'.

Working in the Hungarian archives, Tim realised that 'rather than there being an equal spread of sources from across the country, they were more patchy and also the type of sources differed from place to place'. He calls these records the traces of the Holocaust. Each of these traces tells us about the experience of the Holocaust in that location.

In many ways it is difficult to tell the story of the Holocaust as it was so different in different places and for different people, but the traces found by historians such as Tim help us to understand how individuals experienced this horrific event.

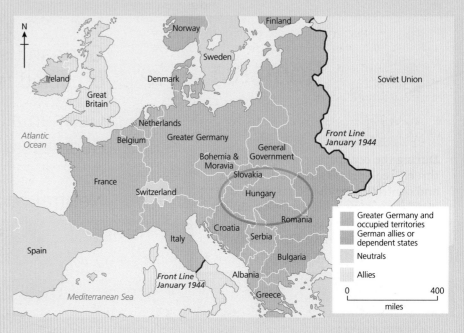

▶ Europe in 1944. Hungary is circled

We cannot look at all of Tim's findings, but three of the traces he has explored are summarised below.

1. The ghetto lists of Veszprém

In the town of Veszprém, the authorities kept extensive lists of the Jews who were kept in ghettos. These lists show that the majority of these people were women. In one particular ghetto, seven out of ten were women, and in the age bracket of 20 to 29 year olds, 97.4 per cent were women.

Where were all the men? In Hungary, Jewish men were called up to the army and forced to serve on the front lines. Conditions for these men were horrific but they did escape the ghettos and the death camps. 'The extent to which the Holocaust was gendered was striking to me. I knew to expect more women than men in the ghettos, but I didn't expect the almost complete lack of adult men that I discovered.'

2. Receipts from Nyíregyháza

In a rural country like Hungary, journeys to and from the ghettos were not always on a train; often they were on horse-drawn carts. The authorities did not have the resources to carry this out on their own and so needed farmers to help.

In Nyíregyháza, receipts were kept of the payments to these people, which help us see the extent of the farmers' involvement. In this one area, 1000 days of cart transport were used between 23 April and 11 May 1944. This involved lots of cart owners from more than 60 different farms.

Large numbers did not just witness this event; they took part. We cannot be sure why the cart owners did this but they were paid very little for their help, so it is unlikely to have been for financial benefit alone.

Reflect

As you read the three traces, think about what they reveal about the Holocaust in each place.

3. A photo from Körmend

▲ Deportation of Jews from Körmend, Hungary, c. June 1944

The photo above was taken in the middle of Körmend, a large town. It shows the deportation of the Jews from the ghetto on their way to take the train to Auschwitz. As you can see, this took place in the middle of the day and was not hidden. Crowds of people are queued up along the street watching the scene.

We do not know who took the photograph or why, but it is a rare glimpse into just one of the awful horrors that were unleashed in Europe in the terrible years when millions were living under Nazi rule.

Preparing for the examination

The world depth study forms the second half of Paper 3: World History. It is worth 20 per cent of your GCSE. To succeed in the examination, you will need to think clearly about different aspects of Living under Nazi Rule, 1933–1945 and support your ideas with accurate knowledge. This section suggests some revision strategies you might like to try and explains the types of examination questions that you can expect.

Summaries of the five key issues

Your study of Living under Nazi Rule, 1933–1945, has covered five important issues:

1. Dictatorship
2. Control and opposition, 1933–1939
3. Changing lives, 1933–1939
4. Germany in war
5. Occupation

In the specification for your GCSE course, each of the five issues is divided into three sections. We divided each enquiry in this book into three stages to match these sections and to help you build your knowledge and understanding step by step.

Now you can use your knowledge and understanding to produce a detailed and accurate summary for each of the five issues. You will also need to be clear about how the five issues are connected. Here are four suggestions for structuring your revision notes and showing the connections between the issues. Choose the one that is best for you, or use a variety if you prefer.

I. Mind maps

A mind map on A3 paper (or even larger) is a good way to summarise the important points about a particular issue. It allows you to show connections between different points.

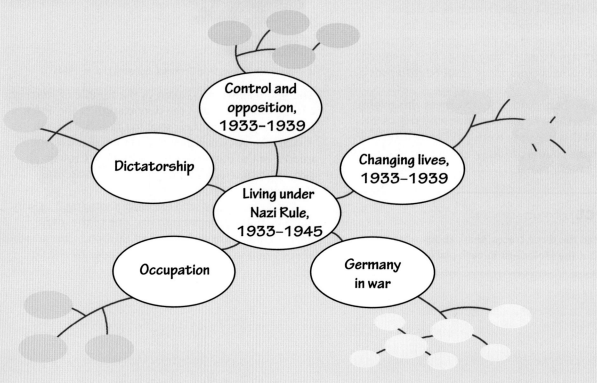

2. Charts

If you find it easier to learn from lists, a summary chart for each issue you have studied might be best for you. You can use the format shown below or design your own. Just make sure that you include clear summary points for each of the three sections in each enquiry you studied.

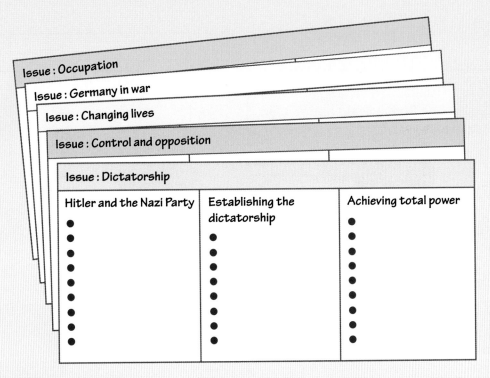

Issue : Occupation

Issue : Germany in war

Issue : Changing lives

Issue : Control and opposition

Issue : Dictatorship

Hitler and the Nazi Party	Establishing the dictatorship	Achieving total power
• • • • • • • •	• • • • • • • •	• • • • • • • •

3. Small cards

Small cards are a flexible way to make revision notes. You could create a set of revision cards for each of the five main issues/enquiries you have studied. It would be a good idea to use a different colour for each set of cards.

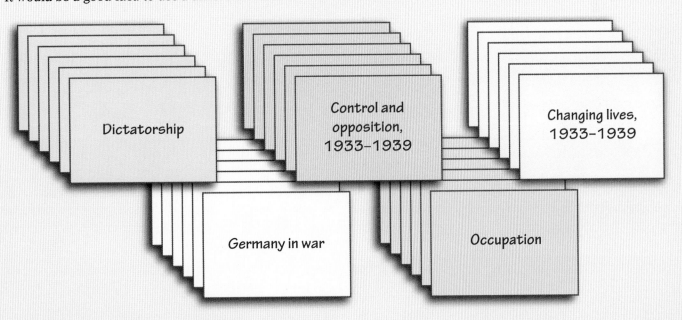

Dictatorship

Control and opposition, 1933–1939

Changing lives, 1933–1939

Germany in war

Occupation

4. Podcasts

If you learn best by listening to information and explanations, you could record your knowledge and understanding by producing podcasts to summarise what you have learned about each of the five main issues. You could produce your podcasts with a friend using a question and answer format.

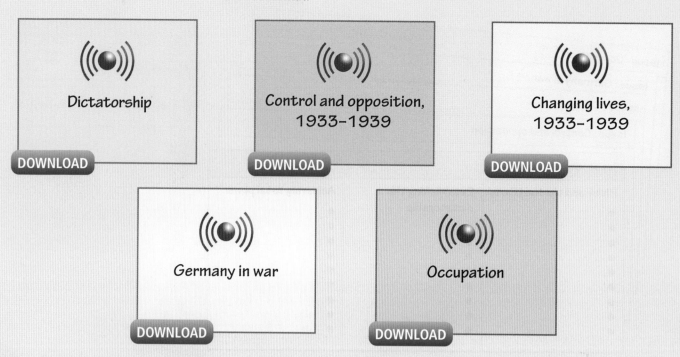

To be well-prepared for the examination you need revision notes that summarise the main points and provide detailed examples in a format that works best for you.

Exam guidance

This depth study forms the second half of Paper 3: World History. It is worth 20 per cent of your GCSE. The whole exam lasts for 1 hour and 45 minutes so you will have just over fifty minutes to answer the three questions on Living under Nazi Rule, 1933–1945.

Question 6

You will be given a single source to analyse. This will focus on an aspect of Living under Nazi Rule that you have studied. The source could be an extract from a written document or an image. The question will always be 'What can Source A tell us about ...' To answer the question you will need to refer to the details in the source and use your own knowledge.

Example

6   What can Source A tell us about Nazi propaganda? Use the source and your own knowledge to support your answer.   (7 marks)

Source A – An announcement in a German newspaper, 16 March 1934

Attention! The Führer will be speaking on the radio. On Wednesday 21 March, the Führer is speaking on all German stations from 11am to 11.50am. The district Party headquarters have ordered that all factory owners, department stores, offices, shops, pubs and blocks of flats put up loudspeakers an hour before the broadcast of the Führer's speech so that the whole workforce and all national comrades can participate fully in the broadcast.

Practise this type of question using the example above.

1. What exactly does this source reveal about:
   ● the types of propaganda used by the Nazis
   ● the features of specific types of propaganda
   ● the ways in which propaganda was produced
   ● the impact of Nazi propaganda?
2. What are the limitations of the source in terms of what it can tell us about Nazi propaganda?
3. Make sure you use some of your own knowledge about Nazi propaganda to analyse the source.

Question 7

You will be given a collection of sources and interpretations to analyse. These could be two sources and an interpretation or two interpretations and a source. The collection will focus on an aspect of Living under Nazi Rule that you have studied. It may include visual, as well as written sources and interpretations. The question stem will always be 'How useful are Interpretation B and sources C and D (or Source B and interpretations C and D) for a historian studying ...? To answer the question you will need to refer to the details in the interpretations and source(s) and use your own knowledge.

Example

7 How useful are Interpretation B and sources C and D for a historian studying the growth of Hitler Youth organisations between 1932 and 1939? In your answer, refer to the interpretation and the two sources as well as your own knowledge.

(15 marks)

Interpretation B – From *The Third Reich in Power* by Richard J. Evans, 2006

From July 1936 the Hitler Youth had an official monopoly on the provision of sports facilities and activities for all children below the age of fourteen; before long, it was the same for 14–18 year olds. In effect, sports facilities were no longer available to non-members. Hitler Youth members were given special days off school for their activities. The results of such pressure soon became apparent. By the end of 1933 there were 2.3 million boys and girls between the ages of ten and eighteen in the Hitler Youth organisation. By the end of 1935 this figure was approaching four million, and by the beginning of 1939 it had reached 8.7 million.

Source C – Graph showing membership numbers of the Hitler Youth organisations, 1932–1939

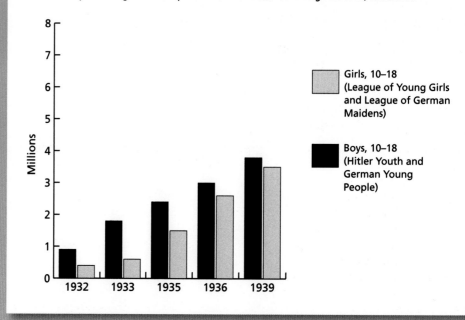

Source D – Poster published by the Nazi government in Germany, 1938. The words on the poster mean: 'Build youth hostels and homes'.

Practise this type of question by using the example above.

1. Make sure you think about the interpretation and sources in relation to the focus of study identified in the question: the growth of Hitler Youth organisations between 1932 and 1939.
2. Study the interpretation and sources carefully and decided what aspects of the growth of Hitler Youth organisations they help us to understand.
3. What exactly do the interpretation and sources tell us about:
   a) the numbers of young people who were members of Hitler Youth organisations in different years
   b) the reasons for the rising numbers
   c) the activities of the Youth organisations?
4. Analyse the interpretation and sources, and use your own knowledge, to think about any limitations in what they can tell us about the growth of Hitler Youth organisations.
5. Make an overall judgement about how useful the interpretation and sources are for a historian studying the growth of Hitler Youth organisations.

Question 8/9

You have a choice of two judgement questions: Question 8 or Question 9. These questions in the second part of Paper 3 are the most challenging because they ask you to make a judgement about an aspect of Living under Nazi Rule, 1933–1939. The question will always ask how far you agree with a given statement. You need to save enough time for this question because it is worth 18 marks.

Examples

8 'There was little effective opposition to the Nazis.' How far do you agree with this view of Germany between 1933 and 1945? **(18 marks)**

9 'German occupation in the Second World War was, in general, far harsher in eastern Europe than in western Europe.' How far do you agree with this view? **(18 marks)**

You may wish to agree completely, disagree completely or take a position where you can see some reasons for agreeing and some for disagreeing. You can get full marks for any of these types of answer provided that you:

- show that you have fully understood the given statement
- use very clear explanations and suitable, accurate supporting evidence to persuade the examiner that you are giving a very reasonable answer
- keep closely to the point all the way through your answer.

Choose one of the example questions above and write a plan of how you would answer it. It is helpful to plan each paragraph in your answer so that it has a very definite main point that is clearly supported with accurate and appropriate evidence chosen from your knowledge of the period.

Copyright information

Interpretation B: Extract from Richard J. Evans, *The Third Reich in Power, 1933 – 1939: How the Nazis Won Over the Hearts and Minds of a Nation*, p 272, Penguin Books Ltd, London, 2006.

Source C: Data from Greg Lacey and Keith Shepherd, *Germany 1918–1945: A depth study: Student's Book (Discovering the Past for GCSE)*, p 130, John Murray Publishers, London, 2002.

Source D: Hitler Youth propaganda poster, 1938 (colour litho), Witte, Herman (fl.1938) / Private Collection / Peter Newark Historical Pictures. Image supplied by Bridgeman Images.

Sources and interpretations

A **source** is a written document, picture, artefact or site which was created by people at the time. Sources such as government documents, diaries, newspapers, photographs, sound recordings, propaganda posters and surviving buildings provide a wealth of evidence about Living under Nazi Rule, 1933–1945.

An **interpretation** is any version of events in the past that has been created at some later time. Interpretations such as books and articles written by historians, documentaries, websites, exhibitions, monuments, novels and films provide a range of different perspectives on Living under Nazi Rule, 1933–1939.

In this book you have studied a wide range of historical sources and interpretations relating to different aspects of Living under Nazi Rule.

1. Select a source from each of the enquiries you have studied. It would be good to choose a mixture of written and visual sources. For each source devise a question 6: 'What can Source X tell us about ...'
2. On pages 76–77 you will find a photograph of Dresden in February 1945 and a written extract from Ian Kershaw's book *The End*. This source and interpretation both shed light on Germany at the end of the war. Do an online search for an additional source (either another photograph or a written source) and then devise a question 7: 'How useful are Interpretation X and sources X and X for a historian studying ...'

Glossary

abolition bringing to an end

anti-Semitic being hostile or prejudiced to Jews

archive a collection of historic documents

Aryans people who settled in northern Europe thousands of years ago. In Nazi belief they were the 'master race'

Atlantic Wall a system of defence built by the Nazis along the coast of Europe between 1942 and 1944

Block Leaders men responsible for Nazi Party activity within a set of about fifty homes in a local area; also known as wardens

boycott to avoid or refuse to have anything to do with a person or business

bunker an underground room used as protection against bombing

Catholics (Roman Catholics) Christians who accept the Pope as the leader of God's Church on Earth

centralise to take power from local people or groups and give it to the national government

Chancellor the term used in Germany for the leader of the government, similar to a British Prime Minister

charisma charm or appeal, strength of personality

chronological in the order in which events happened

civilian a person who is not a member of the armed forces

collaboration when people in an occupied country actively co-operate with the enemy

Communist people who believe that all the people of a community should own its wealth rather than just a few rich individuals or organisations

concentration camp a place where a government forces its enemies to live, under guard and in poor conditions

Concordat an agreement made by the Pope and a government

conscription compulsory service in the armed forces

Conservatives a right-wing political party in Germany that the Nazis believed were too weak

constitution the rules of how a government should work

death camps extermination camps built by the Nazis during the Second World War to kill Jews and others

decree an order

democracy a system where all adults vote to choose those who rule the country

denunciation secretly informing, e.g. telling the Gestapo about what individuals or groups were doing

deport remove someone from a country by force

deputies members of the German Reichstag, like members of Parliament in Britain

Deutsch* or *Deutschen German

dictator a person with complete power

Einsatzgruppen the mobile killing squads that carried out mass murders in the east after 1939

emigrant a person who leaves his or her homeland

evacuation a government scheme for removing children from cities to protect them from bombing

Führer German for 'leader' – in the case of Hitler it meant dictator, the person in total control of Germany

gas chambers air-tight rooms constructed at death camps in which millions of Jews and others were murdered by the Nazis

General Government a German zone of occupation in Poland, established in 1939

Gestapo the secret police in Nazi Germany

ghetto an enclosed area in a city where the Nazis forced Jews to live after 1939

Gleichschaltung the Nazi name for taking control of German society

Head of State the person who represents the nation as its head: in the UK it is the monarch, in Nazi Germany it was the President

Hitlergrüsse the 'Hitler greeting' or salute made with an outstretched arm

Jehovah's Witnesses a religious group whose beliefs stem from Christianity

kommandant a military commander

Länder the regions of Germany

Lebensraum the Nazi policy of taking land from other countries to gain extra 'living space' to keep the German people healthy and wealthy

liberate to free people from imprisonment or occupation

Napola a type of boarding school in Nazi Germany

nationalist a person who believes deeply in keeping a strong, independent nation

Nazi a member of, or the short name for, the *Nationalsozialistische Deutsche Arbeiterpartei* (National Socialist German Workers Party)

occupation the take-over of a territory or country using military force

Orpo ordinary police, i.e. not the secret police (Gestapo)

pastor a Protestant church leader

patriotism a person's pride and love for his or her country

persecute to bully or treat unkindly

propaganda spreading a one-sided message as widely as possible

Protestants Christians who reject the leadership of the Pope and take their lead from what the Bible says

putsch a violent attempt to take over a government

rally a large gathering of enthusiastic supporters

rationing a government system for sharing out available food, fuel and clothes

Reich the German word for 'empire' or 'state'. The Third Reich is the name given to the time when the Nazis ruled Germany, 1933–1945

Reichstag the German Parliament building

Reichswehr the German army

resistance groups of people in occupied countries during the Second World War who attempted to bring an end to Nazi occupation

SA (*Sturmabteilung*) the force that started as a bodyguard for Hitler but became the private army of the Nazi Party. Also known as the Brownshirts

SD (*Sicherheitsdienst*) the Nazi secret service based on spies and informants

Social Democrats a left-wing German political party that opposed the Nazis

SS (*Schutzstaffel*) a relatively small group of highly committed Nazis also known as the Blackshirts. They served as Hitler's bodyguard and were largely responsible for running the Nazi 'machinery of terror'

stormtrooper a member of the SA, also known as a brownshirt

swastika the sign adopted by the Nazi Party and used on flags, armbands, etc.

total war a war which directly involves civilians as well as soldiers

Übermenschen the Nazi word for so-called super humans or the master race, i.e. the Aryans as found in Germany

Untermenschen the Nazi word for so-called sub-human people, notably the Jews

volk or volke the German word for people, e.g. *Dem Deutschen Volke*, the German people

Volkssturm the National Militia

Wannsee Conference the conference at which the Nazis decided to murder all European Jews

Wehrmacht German armed forces (army, navy, air force)

Weimar Government the name of the government that ran Germany from 1918 to 1933. It was hated by the Nazis

Zyklon B the trade name of the cyanide-based insecticide used in gas chambers to murder Jews and others

Index

Acknowledgements

Photo credits

p.6 © INTERFOTO/Alamy Stock Photo; **p.7** © Keystone/ Getty Images; **p.8–9** © Pictorial Press Ltd/Alamy Stock Photo; **p.10–11** © The Print Collector/Print Collector/ Getty Images; **p.12** Event against the Treaty of Versailles at a school in Berlin, 1933 (b/w photo)/© SZ Photo/Scherl/ Bridgeman Images; **p.14** © World History Archive/Alamy Stock Photo; **p.15** © Imagno/Getty Images; **p.16** *t* © Pahl, Georg - Bundesarchiv, *b* © ullstein bild via Getty Images; **p.18** *t* © World History Archive/Alamy Stock Photo, *b* © Mary Evans Picture Library/Alamy Stock Photo; **p.19** © INTERFOTO/Alamy Stock Photo; **p.20** © akg-images/ Alamy Stock Photo; **p.21** *t* © Frederick Bass/Getty Images, *b* © Archiv Gerstenberg/ullstein bild via Getty Images; **p.23** *t* © Keystone/Getty Images, *c* © Pictorial Press Ltd/ Alamy Stock Photo; **p.24** © The Print Collector/Alamy Stock Photo; **p.25** *t* © akg-images, *c* © akg-images, *b* © akg-images; **p.26** © Mary Evans/SZ Photo/Scherl; **p.27** © World History Archive/Alamy Stock Photo; **p.28** © bpk/Heinrich Hoffmann; **p.30** *t* © ullstein bild/ullstein bild via Getty Images, *b* © ullstein bild/ullstein bild via Getty Images; **p.31** © Yad Vashem; **p.32** *t* © AF archive/Alamy Stock Photo, *b* © John Frost Newspapers/Alamy Stock Photo; **p.33** *t* © INTERFOTO/Alamy Stock Photo, *b* © FPG/Hulton Archive/Getty Images; **p.34–35** background © Marshall Ikonography/Alamy Stock Photo; **p.34** *l* © Prisma Bildagentur AG/Alamy Stock Photo, *r* © Galerie Bilderwelt/ Getty Images; **p.35** *tl* © Glasshouse Images/Alamy Stock Photo, *tr* © ushmm.org, *br* © Prisma Bildagentur AG/Alamy Stock Photo, *br* © Peter Horree/Alamy Stock Photo; **p.36** *t* © ullstein bild/ullstein bild via Getty Images, *b* © bpk/ Kunstbibliothek, SMB; **p.38** © dpa picture alliance/Alamy Stock Photo; **p.39** *Niemoller* © Walter Sanders/The LIFE Picture Collection/Getty Images, *Pope Pius XI* © World History Archive/Alamy Stock Photo, *Cardinal Galen* © Borgas/ullstein bild via Getty Images, *b* © United States Holocaust Memorial Museum; **p.41** © ullstein bild via Getty Images; **p.42** *t* Sunflowers, 1932 (oil on canvas), Nolde, Emil (1867–1956)/Detroit Institute of Arts, USA/Gift of Robert H. Tannahill/Bridgeman Images; **p.43** © EMIL NOLDE STIFTUNG,SEEBUELL,GERMANY via LESSING IMAGES; **p.44** © Farming Family from Kalenberg, 1939 (oil on canvas), Wissel, Adolf (1894–1973)/Property of the Federal Republic of Germany/Bridgeman Images; **p.46** © Everett Historical – Shutterstock; **p.47** *t* © Heinrich Hoffmann/ ullstein bild via Getty Images, *b* © Bettmann/Getty Images; **p.48** © Mary Evans Picture Library/Alamy Stock Photo; **p.49** © Stephen French/Alamy Stock Photo; **p.51** © ullstein bild/ullstein bild via Getty Images); **p.52** © bnps.co.uk; **p.53** *t* © INTERFOTO/Alamy Stock Photo, *b* © INTERFOTO/ Alamy Stock Photo; **p.54** *t* © bpk | Michael Sobotta, *b* © Deutsches Historisches Museum, Berlin; **p.55** © World

History Archive/Alamy Stock Photo; **p.56** *t* © Dorothy Alexander/Alamy Stock Photo, *c* © Heinrich Sanden/ Deutsches Bundesarchiv (https://commons.wikimedia.org/ wiki/File:Bundesarchiv_Bild_146-1971-006- 02,_München,_ Judenverfolgung,_Michael_Siegel.jpg), *b* © United States Holocaust Memorial Museum; **p.57** *background* © Sergio Azenha/Stockimo/Alamy Stock Photo, *b* © Granger Historical Picture Archive/Alamy Stock Photo; **p.60–61** © ullstein bild/ullstein bild via Getty Images; **p.62** © ZUMA Press, Inc./Alamy Stock Photo; **p.63** © Eden Breitz/Alamy Stock Photo; **p.64** *t* © akg-images, *b* © Photos 12/Alamy Stock Photo; **p.65** Photo © Everett Collection/Bridgeman Images; **p.66** © Deutsches Historisches Museum, Berlin; **p.67** *t* © World History Archive/Alamy Stock Photo, *b* © dpa picture alliance/Alamy Stock Photo; **p.68** © Keystone Pictures USA/Alamy Stock Photo; **p.69** *t* © Borgas/ullstein bild via Getty Images, *c* © Granger Historical Picture Archive/Alamy Stock Photo, *b* © Photos 12/Alamy Stock Photo; **p.70** *t* © Aufbau Verlag via Wikimedia Commons (https://en.wikipedia.org/wiki/File:Hampel_postcard. jpg), *b* © Authenticated News/Archive Photos/Getty Images; **p.72** © Mary Evans/Sueddeutsche Zeitung Photo; **p.73** © Peter Horree/Alamy Stock Photo; **p.74** *t* © Scherl – Bundesarchiv, *b* © Deutsches Historisches Museum, Berlin; **p.75** *t* © United States Holocaust Memorial Museum, *b* © o. Ang. – Bundesarchiv; **p.76** © Prisma Bildagentur AG/Alamy Stock Photo; **p.77** *l* © dpa picture alliance archive/Alamy Stock Photo, *r* © *The End* by Ian Kershaw 978-0141014210 © Penguin; **p.78** © Pictorial Press Ltd/Alamy Stock Photo; **p.79** *t* © dpa picture alliance/Alamy Stock Photo, *b* © dpa picture alliance/Alamy Stock Photo; **p.80** © Popperfoto/ Getty Images; **p. 82** © Everett Collection Historical/Alamy Stock Photo; **p.83** *t* © World History Archive/Alamy Stock Photo, *b* © IMAGEPAST/Alamy Stock Photo; **p.84** *t* © World History Archive/Alamy Stock Photo *b* © World History Archive/Alamy Stock Photo; **p.85** *t* and *b* © Pieter Boersma – Dutch Resistance Museum; **p.86** *t* © Heritage Image Partnership Ltd/Alamy Stock Photo, *b* © epa european pressphoto agency b.v./Alamy Stock Photo; **p.87** *c* © Mary Evans/Sueddeutsche Zeitung Photo; **p.88** *t* © United States Holocaust Memorial Museum, *b* © RIA Novosti/TopFoto; **p.90** *l* © akg-images/Alamy Stock Photo; **p.90–91** © akg-images/Alamy Stock Photo; **p.91** *r* © Michael Regan – The FA/The FA via Getty Images; **p.92** © Josse Christophel/ Alamy Stock Photo; **p.93** *b* © Pictorial Press Ltd/Alamy Stock Photo; **p.96** Photograph courtesy of Tim Cole; **p.97** © Unknown photographer/Collection of the Hungarian National Museum; **p.103** © Hitler Youth propaganda poster, 1938 (colour litho), Witte, Herman (fl.1938)/Private Collection/Peter Newark Historical Pictures/Bridgeman Images.